SPiN

Workbook

2

Catherine Milton

Spin 2 Workbook

Catherine Milton

Publisher: Gavin McLean

Director of Content Development: Sarah Bideleux

Managing Editor: Angela Cussons

Art Director: Natasa Arsenidou

Cover Designer: Natasa Arsenidou

Text Designer / Compositor: Sofia Fourtouni

National Geographic Liaison: Leila Hishmeh

Acknowledgements

Editorial management by Process ELT / Georgia Zographou

ISBN: 978-1-4080-6103-9

National Geographic Learning

Cheriton House, North Way, Andover, Hampshire, SP10 5BE
United Kingdom

Cengage Learning is a leading provider of customized learning solutions with office locations around the globe, including Singapore, the United Kingdom, Australia, Mexico, Brazil and Japan. Locate your local office at: **international.cengage.com/region**

Cengage Learning products are represented in Canada by Nelson Education, Ltd.

Visit National Geographic Learning online at **ngl.cengage.com**
Visit our corporate website at **www.cengage.com**

Photo credits

Cover image: Brian Skerry/NGIC. A school of juvenile marine catfish masses over the sandy bottom of Suruga Bay off Japan's Izu Peninsula.

3-18 (all) Shutterstock, **20-31** (all) Shutterstock, **32** Gary Brennand/NGIC, **34-39** (all) Shutterstock, **41-46** (all) Shutterstock, **48-59** (all) Shutterstock, **60** George Grall/NGIC, **62-73** (all) Shutterstock, **74** Jason Tucker/NGIC, **76-87** (all) Shutterstock, **88** Lori Epstein/NGIC

NGIC = National Geographic Image Collection

Printed in the United Kingdom by Ashford Colour Press Ltd.

Print Number: 14   Print Year: 2023

Contents

Introduction

Vocabulary

1 Match.

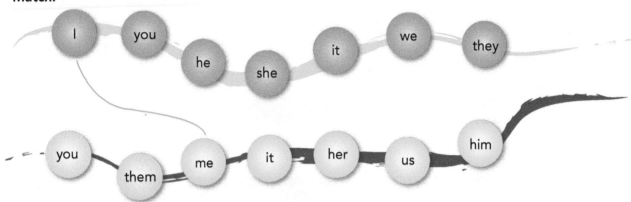

I · you · he · she · it · we · they

you · them · me · it · her · us · him

2 Circle the correct words.

1 This is Kristie's marker. She bought (it) / him this morning.
2 There are Jim and Louise. Let's go and play with us / them.
3 I'm writing to my aunt. I write to him / her every week.
4 We're skateboarding. Look at us / them!
5 This present is for them / you. Happy birthday!
6 This is Peter's pizza. It's for him / me.

3 Complete the sentences with these words.

her its my our their your

1 I'm thirteen and _____ my _____ sister is ten.
2 We have got a big bedroom with all _____ toys in it.
3 Carla and Ryan are staying with _____ grandmother this weekend.
4 I can't believe Marie is _____ sister. She doesn't look like you.
5 The dog is looking for _____ bone.
6 This is Sharon's invitation. It's for _____.

4 Complete the sentences with the correct form of there is or there are.

1 _____Is there_____ a dolphin in the water?

2 Look! _____ a car in our garden.

3 No, _____ a phone in the house.

4 _____ any animals in the park?

5 I'm sorry, but _____ any books for you.

6 _____ lots of children in the classroom.

5 Choose the correct answers.

1 __ do you do on Saturdays?
  a When
  b Who
  c What

2 __ does Jim go to school?
  a What
  b Where
  c Whose

3 __ hat is this?
  a Who
  b What
  c Whose

4 __ at the door?
  a When
  b Who's
  c Whose

5 __ do you have lunch?
  a What
  b When
  c Who

6 __ did you buy at the shops?
  a Who
  b Where
  c What

6 Look at the picture and write sentences with There is or There are and prepositions of place.

1 a clock / the glass of milk
  There is a clock behind the glass of milk.
  _____

2 two eggs / the clock
  _____
  _____

3 a cup of coffee / the bread and the cereal
  _____
  _____

4 an egg / the glass of milk
  _____
  _____

5 two drinks / the picture
  _____
  _____

6 an apple / the picture
  _____
  _____

Vocabulary

1 **Complete the sentences with these words.**

aunt cousin grandchildren nephews only wife

1 That's my dad's sister. She is my _____*aunt*_____.
2 Beth isn't a(n) _____ child – she's got a brother.
3 Those are my brother's sons. They are my _____.
4 This is Mr Philips and that is Mrs Philips, his _____.
5 That's not my sister. She's my _____ – my uncle's daughter.
6 My grandmother has got two _____, my brother and me!

2 **Circle the correct words.**

1 Jim and Nick are my aunt's sons. They're my nephews / cousins.
2 Don't shout at me in front of my friends. It's alone / embarrassing.
3 My mum is from Germany and we've got relatives / families there.
4 Jane and Paula are my nieces / nephews.
5 My grandparents are on holiday and I really meet / miss them.

3 **Match.**

1 Are you Greek?
2 Is this a normal globe?
3 Can you do Kristie a favour?
4 Is that girl your daughter?
5 Can I use your laptop?

a No, it's magic!
b Sure. I don't need it now.
c Of course I can.
d That's right.
e No, she's my niece.

Grammar

4 Complete the sentences with the Present Simple of the verbs in brackets.

1 Does your mother _____ *work* _____ (work) at weekends?

2 It _____ (not rain) a lot in Greece.

3 Beth _____ (want) to go back home.

4 She _____ (visit) her aunt on Sundays.

5 _____ Kristie and Mikey _____ (like) travelling?

6 We _____ (not get up) early on Saturdays.

7 Ms Dean _____ (teach) maths.

8 He _____ (go) on holiday in the winter.

5 Choose the correct answers.

1 Do they ___ here?
   (a) live
   b lives
   c doesn't live

2 Mikey and Kristie ___ their magic globe.
   a not like
   b likes
   c like

3 'Do you visit your grandparents on Saturdays?' 'Yes, ___.'
   a they do
   b we do
   c she does

4 Adam always ___ his camera with him.
   a carry
   b carries
   c does carry

5 Steve ___ get up early on Saturdays.
   a doesn't
   b not
   c don't

6 Does it usually ___ in Amsterdam in winter?
   a don't snow
   b snows
   c snow

6 Put the adverbs of frequency in brackets in the correct place.

1 My family is nice to me. (always)
   My family is always nice to me.

2 The three o'clock train is late. (never)
   _____
   _____

3 Beth doesn't visit her cousins. (often)
   _____
   _____

4 Grandma helps me with my homework. (usually)
   _____
   _____

5 Mum is embarrassing. (sometimes)
   _____
   _____

6 Do Mikey and Kristie travel through time? (sometimes)
   _____
   _____

Vocabulary

1 **Circle the correct words.**

1 The baby albatross isn't safe / long on its own.
2 Let's look at my video team / diary!
3 These birds fly long turns / distances to find food.
4 I'm looking for / taking care of Dad. Do you know where he is?
5 Albatrosses are birds with big wings / pairs.

2 **Complete the crossword puzzle.**

Across

1 Both _____parents_____ look after their babies.
6 They've got a(n) _____ of rabbits in their garden.
7 I want to _____ some time with Mum this weekend.

Down

2 The _____ is a white sea bird.
3 The mother albatross is sitting on the egg – she's keeping it _____ and safe.
4 It can _____ its wings, but it can't fly!
5 How often do you _____ your pet snake?

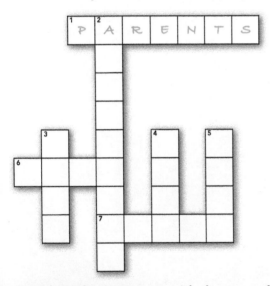

3 **Complete the sentences with these words.**

after   at   for (x2)   of   on

1 I don't like spending time ___on___ my own.
2 Do mother and father albatrosses stay together _____ life?
3 Kristie is looking _____ the globe. Where is it?
4 She's feeding the cat _____ the moment.
5 Both parents look _____ their babies.
6 Mikey is taking care _____ Beth's cat today.

8

Grammar

4 Complete the sentences with the Present Continuous of these verbs. Use the affirmative or negative form.

chase feed fly rain visit watch

1 I ____'m /am not feeding____ the cat now – it's not hungry. ✗
2 We _____ our favourite programme on TV. ✓
3 She _____ her cousin in Oxford today. ✗
4 Help! A dog _____ my cat! ✓
5 The baby birds _____! Look at their small wings! ✓
6 It _____ today – it's nice and sunny! ✗

5 Put the words in the correct order to make sentences.

1 a board game / are / Adam and Beth / now / playing
   Adam and Beth are playing a board game now.

2 isn't / his cousin / today / visiting / he
   _____

3 ? / is / the video diary / watching / this morning / Tom
   _____

4 ? / you / looking after / are / today / your brother
   _____

5 spinning / at the moment / isn't / the globe
   _____

6 are / now / their wings / the puffins / moving
   _____

6 Look at the pictures and write questions and short answers with the Present Continuous.

? / the albatrosses / fly
Are the albatrosses flying?
No, they aren't.

? / they / watch / TV
_____
_____

? / Ann / feed / her dog
_____
_____

? / Sue / look for / her mobile phone
_____
_____

? / the dog / sleep
_____
_____

? / the boy / travel / by plane
_____
_____

9

Lesson 3

Vocabulary

1 **Complete the sentences with these words.**

building   fashion   grow up   mad   miss   rude

1 My sister is funny, but she is very _____rude_____ sometimes!
2 That's an interesting _____! Let's take a photo.
3 My cousin wants to be a _____ photographer.
4 When I _____, I want to work in a French restaurant.
5 I really _____ my parents – I want to go home!
6 Kevin is _____ about rollerblading.

Grammar

2 **Choose the correct answers.**

1 Miranda ___ her pets.
  a is loving
  b loving
  ⓒ loves

2 Jessica ___ photos at the moment.
  a taking
  b is taking
  c take

3 Mabel and Karen ___ in Canada.
  a live
  b are living
  c lives

4 Allison always ___ long hours.
  a is working
  b works
  c aren't working

5 I ___ like rollerblading.
  a am not
  b doesn't
  c don't

6 The twins ___ tennis at the moment.
  a don't play
  b aren't playing
  c play

7 He ___ his cousins now.
  a visits
  b are visiting
  c is visiting

8 I don't ___ what to do.
  a understanding
  b not understanding
  c understand

Express yourself!

3 **Match.**

1 You look horrible in that dress, Mrs Johnson!
2 Look at my new MP3 player.
3 She falls asleep when we go to the cinema.
4 This is my baby brother.
5 Your cat eats a lot!

  a It's so embarrassing!
  b It's so fat!
  c It's so cool!
  d You're so rude!
  e He's so cute!

Writing

4 **Read the description of Sharon's family and circle the correct words.**

Hi! My name's Sharon and this is my family.

I'm thirteen years old and I have got an older brother. I love playing tennis. I **(1)** now / usually have tennis lessons **(2)** this morning / on Saturdays. But **(3)** this / every Saturday we are going on holiday to Spain. Our cousins live there!

My cousins, Pedro and Eva, are a lot of fun. They **(4)** today / always do exciting things. We love rollerblading, so we **(5)** never / sometimes go to the rollerblading park near their house.

My mum and dad love Spain, too. They like swimming and when they are in Spain they go to the beach **(6)** every day / at the moment.

We've also got a cat called Blackie, but you can't see him in this photo. He's at home!

Remember!

We use these adverbs of frequency with the Present Simple: always, usually, often, sometimes, never.

We use these time expressions with the Present Simple: every day/week/weekend/ spring/summer/autumn/winter, once a week/month/year, at the weekends.

We use these time expressions with the Present Continuous: this morning/spring/ summer/autumn/winter, next week/month/ year, now, at the moment, today, tomorrow.

5 **Write a description of your best friend's family. Use this plan to help you.**

Paragraph 1
Introduce your best friend and say why you like him/her.

Paragraph 2
Write about your best friend's brother(s) or sister(s), his/her aunt/ uncle/cousins, etc.

Paragraph 3
Write about your friend's parents.

Paragraph 4
Write about your friend's pet.

Vocabulary

1 Label the pictures with these words.

| bedroom | coffee table | kitchen | palace | sink | stairs |

1 _____kitchen_____ 2 _____ 3 _____

4 _____ 5 _____ 6 _____

2 Find seven house-related words. Then use these words to complete the sentences.

```
U H B J E H I D Q J
B T W I N D O W X W
Y J A Q P T K S X O
D B R K E X A F T E
R N D P J S L R H G
U A R M C H A I R D
Z S O F A O K D D N
A V B N C W O G G V
O V E N Q E F E X M
J G U K T R C D U H
```

1 Please close the ____window____. I'm cold.
2 This is grandpa's favourite _____ – he always sits there.
3 Put the pizza in the _____ for 20 minutes.
4 Where's my white shirt? It's not in my _____.
5 The girls are sitting on the _____ and they're watching TV.
6 She opened the _____ and looked for something to eat.
7 I always get in the _____ at 6.30 am, before breakfast.

3 Match.

1 Why is your face red?
2 Why did Mr Peterson shout at you?
3 Did you visit the palace?
4 How many people work here?
5 When did Christopher Columbus live?

a I was late for class again.
b In the 15th century.
c We have a staff of twenty people.
d Yes, it was impressive!
e I climbed up a lot of stairs!

Grammar

4 Complete the sentences with the Past Simple of the verbs in brackets.

Erica: Wow! Your new room is fantastic!

Kelly: I know. I **(1)** ___moved___ (move) in here last week. I **(2)** _____ (want) a cool room and now I've got it.

Erica: You've got pink furniture and pink walls!

Kelly: Yes, Mum and Dad **(3)** _____ (paint) them. Do you like pink?

Erica: Yes, pink is one of my favourite colours. Your room is so tidy.

Kelly: I **(4)** _____ (tidy) it this morning. My little sister **(5)** _____ (help) too. I love my new room!

5 Rewrite the sentences in the negative form of the Past Simple.

1 We arrived at the palace at 5 o'clock.
   We didn't arrive at the palace at 5 o'clock.

2 They looked for new furniture yesterday.
   _____

3 She wanted a huge swimming pool.
   _____

4 He shouted at his baby brother.
   _____

5 We cleaned the kitchen this morning.
   _____

6 Mikey opened the fridge.
   _____

7 It rained all last week.
   _____

8 You stayed with your aunt last summer.
   _____

6 Look at the pictures and write questions and short answers with the Past Simple.

? / Maria / watch / TV / last night
Did Maria watch TV last night?
No, she didn't.

? / they / paint / the walls green
_____

? / they / climb up / the stairs
_____

? / I / tidy / my bedroom
_____

? / Andreas / stay / at home
_____

? / you / cook / dinner / last night
_____

Vocabulary

1 **Circle the correct words.**

1 We used a **bucket** / camera to carry water.
2 I live on the second **place** / **floor**.
3 The **temple** / **roof** had high stone walls.
4 The house was old, but it had **running** / **tasty** water.
5 Put your dirty clothes in the washing **room** / **machine**, please.

2 **Write the missing letters.**

1 You put these on the windows.   c <u>u r t a i n s</u>
2 This is a piece of furniture with shelves for books.   b _ _ _ _ _ _ _
3 This is the top of a building.   r _ _ _
4 You look at this and see yourself in it.   m _ _ _ _ _
5 We put this on the floor to keep the room warm.   r _ _

3 **Complete the paragraph with these words.**

balcony   floor   huge   magical   mirrors   wooden

I remember my grandmother's house in Scotland. It was a truly **(1)** ___magical___
place for me! It was **(2)** _____ and had two floors. It had a sitting room
with **(3)** _____ furniture and beautiful rugs. There were paintings and
(4) _____ on the walls. There were three big bedrooms on the second
(5) _____. My bedroom had a small **(6)** _____ with a beautiful
view. Every afternoon, we had tea on the balcony and Grandma told me stories
about ghosts in Scottish castles.

Grammar

4 **Complete the sentences with the Past Simple of the verbs in brackets.**

1 Mark _____put_____ (put) water in the bucket.
2 We all _____ (drink) tea in the afternoon.
3 They _____ (sleep) on the roof on hot nights.
4 The children _____ (eat) snacks.
5 She _____ (write) me an email last week.
6 They _____ (take) photos of temples and palaces.

5 **Complete the sentences with the Past Simple of these verbs.**

| become buy come ~~give~~ go grow up sell |

1 We _____gave_____ them our old washing machine.
2 It was hot so we _____ to the beach for a swim.
3 My parents _____ me furniture from a new shop in town.
4 We met in India and we _____ best friends.
5 She _____ in Australia.
6 He _____ his cottage and moved to a flat.
7 My grandmother _____ from a small town in India.

6 **Write sentences in the Past Simple.**

1 Sally / catch / the ball
   Sally caught the ball.

2 David / buy / a vacuum cleaner
   _____

3 we / spend / a week / in Italy
   _____

4 Mum and Dad / sit / on the balcony
   _____

5 I / meet / my friends
   _____

6 Grandpa / read / a story
   _____

Vocabulary

1 Look at the pictures and write the missing letters.

s i t t i n g   r o o m   h _ _ _ _ _ _ _ _   c _ _ _ _ _ _

f _ _ _   h _ _   v _ _ _ _ _ _

Speaking

2 Make a list of the furniture in your bedroom.

_____

_____

_____

_____

_____

_____

_____

_____

_____

3 Tell your partner about your bedroom.

Express yourself!

4 Complete the dialogue with these words.

flat   live   modern   move   village

Eric: Where do you **(1)** _____ live _____, Danny?

Danny: I live in a huge **(2)** _____ in the city.

Eric: Cool! You're near all the theatres and shopping centres.

Danny: That's right. I like it there. I lived in an old cottage in a small **(3)** _____ before. It was really boring.

Eric: When did you **(4)** _____ in?

Danny: I moved into the flat a year ago.

Eric: Is the flat **(5)** _____?

Danny: Yes, it is. It's only one year old. Why don't you come and see it next weekend?

Writing

5 Circle the correct words.

HOUSE TO RENT!

This beautiful house is in the city centre **(1)** so / because you can walk to cinemas, restaurants and shopping centres! It's a great home for young people. It's got two bedrooms **(2)** and / but a huge sitting room. You can cook all your meals there **(3)** so / because there's a great modern kitchen. It hasn't got a balcony **(4)** but / and it's got a fantastic garden. The house is old **(5)** but / and all the furniture is new. You can live in this house **(6)** but / and enjoy life in the city!

Remember!

Linking words make our writing better.
- **and** adds something else to a sentence
- **but** shows that something is different to another thing
- **because** gives the reason for something
- **so** gives the result of something

The flat is huge and modern.
The house is beautiful but old.
I changed schools because I moved house.
They live in London so they speak English.

6 Write an advert for your dream house. Use this plan to help you.

Answer the questions:

What kind of house is it?

Where is it?

Who can live in it?

How many rooms are there?

What are they?

Is the house old or new?

Is the furniture modern/wooden/old?

What can you do there?

17

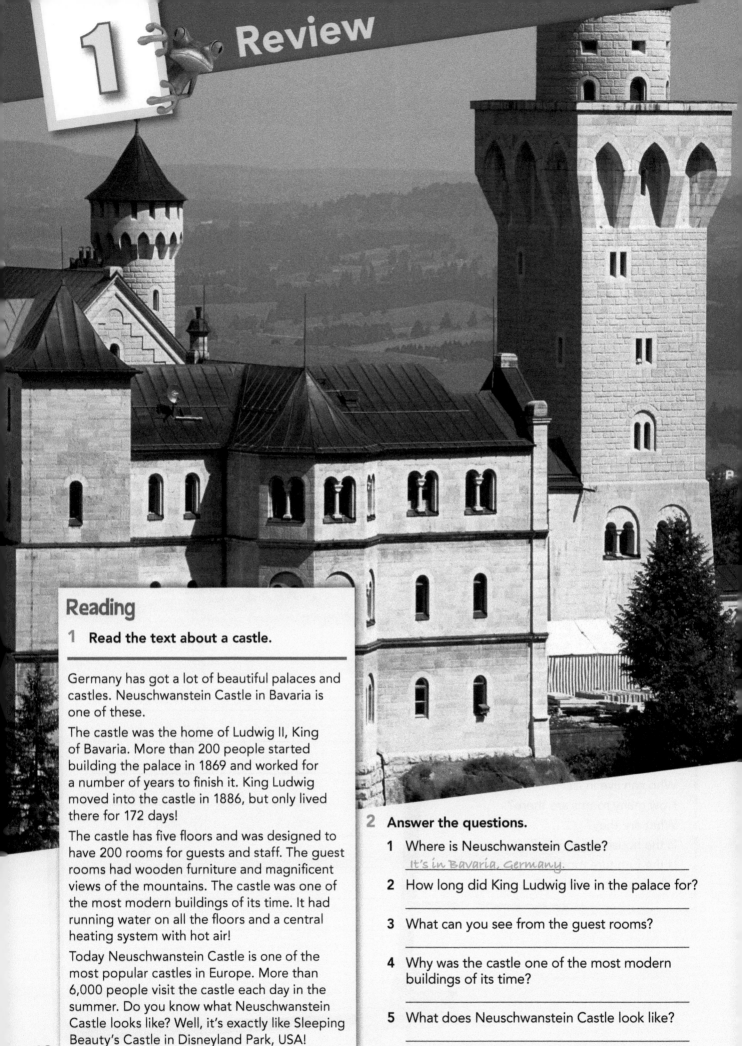

Reading

1 Read the text about a castle.

Germany has got a lot of beautiful palaces and castles. Neuschwanstein Castle in Bavaria is one of these.

The castle was the home of Ludwig II, King of Bavaria. More than 200 people started building the palace in 1869 and worked for a number of years to finish it. King Ludwig moved into the castle in 1886, but only lived there for 172 days!

The castle has five floors and was designed to have 200 rooms for guests and staff. The guest rooms had wooden furniture and magnificent views of the mountains. The castle was one of the most modern buildings of its time. It had running water on all the floors and a central heating system with hot air!

Today Neuschwanstein Castle is one of the most popular castles in Europe. More than 6,000 people visit the castle each day in the summer. Do you know what Neuschwanstein Castle looks like? Well, it's exactly like Sleeping Beauty's Castle in Disneyland Park, USA!

2 Answer the questions.

1 Where is Neuschwanstein Castle?
  It's in Bavaria, Germany.

2 How long did King Ludwig live in the palace for?
  _____

3 What can you see from the guest rooms?
  _____

4 Why was the castle one of the most modern buildings of its time?
  _____

5 What does Neuschwanstein Castle look like?
  _____

Vocabulary

3 Choose the correct answers.

1 Can you do me a ___, please?
   a favour
   b turn
   c diary

2 Grandma always sits in her favourite ___ next to the fireplace.
   a oven
   b coffee table
   c armchair

3 How many times a day do you ___ your pet rabbit?
   a miss
   b feed
   c shout

4 King Ludwig II lived in the 19th ___.
   a temple
   b palace
   c century

5 Albatross parents always take care ___ their babies.
   a for
   b of
   c after

6 Can I use your ___? I need to clean the sitting room.
   a vacuum cleaner
   b rug
   c sink

7 I can't ask her to invite me – it's a little ___!
   a safe
   b embarrassing
   c normal

8 We slept on the ___ last night – it was too hot in the house.
   a curtain
   b roof
   c mirror

9 The palace had a ___ of 200 people.
   a staff
   b guest
   c sword

10 Those birds fly long ___ over the sea.
   a distances
   b wings
   c diaries

11 My grandmother's house had beautiful ___ furniture.
   a huge
   b alone
   c wooden

12 The little boy over there is my sister's son – he's my ___.
   a niece
   b wife
   c nephew

Grammar

4 Choose the correct answers.

1 Mum ___ on Friday nights.
   a works always
   b always works
   c always working

2 ___ after the twins at the weekends?
   a Grandma looks
   b Does Grandma look
   c Grandma doesn't look

3 'Does it rain here in winter?' 'Yes, ___.'
   a it rains
   b it does
   c it is

4 Look! Those birds ___ over the sea!
   a fly
   b flying
   c are flying

5 'Is your little brother sleeping at the moment?' 'No, ___.'
   a he doesn't
   b he doesn't sleep
   c he isn't

6 I was late but they ___ shout at me.
   a didn't
   b not
   c don't

7 Did you ___ your bedroom last night?
   a tidied
   b tidies
   c tidy

8 What are you doing ___?
   a tomorrow
   b at the weekends
   c every day

9 Did you ___ that noise?
   a heard
   b hearing
   c hear

10 Ben ___ Neuschwanstein Castle last year.
   a sees
   b is seeing
   c saw

11 Donna ___ some new furniture for her bedroom last week.
   a bought
   b buys
   c is buying

12 Did he ___ to bed late last night?
   a went
   b goes
   c go

Vocabulary

1 **Complete the dialogue with these words.**

> brilliant competition fault practise skater way

Patrick: Hi, Diana! What are you doing here? Are you taking part in the ice-skating
(1) ___competition___ at 3 o'clock?

Diana: No, I'm not. I'm here to (2) _____. I want to become a really
good (3) _____!

Patrick: I was here when you were practising last week and I thought you were
(4) _____!

Diana: Thanks, Patrick! I fell once or twice, but it wasn't my (5) _____
. Peter Smiley pushed me!

Patrick: That wasn't very nice of him. Oh, by the (6) _____, do you
want to go to the cinema with me on Friday?

Diana: Sure!

2 **Complete the sentences with these words.**

> give go keep take try

1 Why don't you _____take_____ up a new hobby? What about tennis?

2 Steve, don't _____ up! You can do it!

3 Can I _____ out your new computer game? It looks cool!

4 Don't stop now, Sophia. _____ on trying!

5 When did you _____ off tennis? You loved the sport last week!

3 **Match.**

1 Did they win the match?
2 Be careful, Adam!
3 What's your new hobby?
4 We are awful at this!
5 My name's Steven, by the way.
6 Let's go back home.

a Why? Aren't you having fun?
b Collecting stamps.
c Sorry! I wasn't looking.
d You're right. Let's try again.
e I think so.
f Hi! I'm Diana.

Grammar

4 **Choose the correct answers.**

1 He wasn't ice-skating ___.
   a at three o'clock yesterday
   b next Thursday
   c at the moment

2 Were ___ baseball yesterday afternoon?
   a they playing
   b they play
   c playing

3 What were you doing from 2 o'clock ___ 6 o'clock yesterday?
   a at
   b till
   c on

4 Adam ___ with Mikey and Kristie.
   a were skating
   b skating
   c was skating

5 'Were the girls having lunch at 12 o'clock yesterday?'
   a 'Yes, they are.'
   b 'Yes, they did.'
   c 'Yes, they were.'

5 **Rewrite the sentences in the negative form of the Past Continuous.**

1 Diana was dancing with Adam last Saturday.
   Diana wasn't dancing with Adam last Saturday.

2 We were skating all morning.
   _____

3 The boys were surfing at 6 o'clock yesterday morning.
   _____

4 I was swimming at the pool yesterday afternoon.
   _____

5 He was practising for the game till 3 o'clock.
   _____

6 You were sending emails last night.
   _____

6 **Look at the pictures and write questions and short answers with the Past Continuous.**

1 ? / the girls / skate / yesterday morning
   Were the girls skating yesterday morning?
   Yes, they were.

2 ? / Paul / swim / at this time yesterday
   _____
   _____

3 ? / the boys / ride their bikes / this morning
   _____
   _____

4 ? / Ann / listen to music / yesterday afternoon
   _____
   _____
   _____

5 ? / Josh / play tennis / this morning
   _____
   _____
   _____

6 ? / Bob / study / last night at nine o'clock
   _____
   _____
   _____

3 Lesson 2

Vocabulary

1 Complete the paragraph with these words.

activity ~~bored~~ entertaining hill scared take up

COME TUBING!

Are you **(1)** ____bored____ of computer games? Do
you want to **(2)** _____ a new sport? Why don't
you try tubing? Tubing is like skiing, but it's more fun!
You ride in a ring that has got a hole in it. You can slide
down a(n) **(3)** _____ or even fly through the
air! Don't be **(4)** _____! Tubing is easy to learn
and it's very **(5)** _____! It's a great winter
(6) _____ for all the family!

Call 208 345 7865 now!

2 Complete the sentences with the correct adjectives.

excited   exciting

1 We're going camping tomorrow! I'm really _____excited_____!
2 Tubing is a very _____exciting_____ activity!

tired   tiring

3 Skiing is fun, but it's also very _____.
4 I feel so _____ after walking up the hill!

bored   boring

5 Chris is never _____ in her free time. She has lots of hobbies.
6 This board game is _____. Let's go and make a snowman!

interested   interesting

7 This is a very _____ article about insects.
8 I'm not _____ in winter sports.

3 Circle the correct words.

1 Let's make / do a snowman!
2 Stop! Don't throw / step snowballs at me!
3 You don't need expensive exercise / equipment for ice-skating.
4 Skiing is a lot of fun! It's more entertaining / boring than climbing.
5 Look! He's throwing / sliding down the hill!
6 Put on / Step your snowshoes and let's go!

Grammar

4 **Circle the correct words.**

1 I wasn't skiing down the hill when I (fell) / was falling down.
2 It was snowing when they were arriving / arrived at the airport.
3 I was cooking dinner when / while John called.
4 Was Ron playing basketball when the rain was starting / started?
5 While she was walking / walked home, her mobile phone rang.

5 **Complete the sentences with the Past Simple or the Past Continuous of the verbs in brackets.**

1 She was swimming when she _____ saw _____ (see) a shark.
2 They _____ (not play) baseball when it started to rain.
3 We were reading our emails when we _____ (hear) the doorbell.
4 He _____ (put on) his shoes when the phone rang.
5 What _____ (you/do) when I called you?
6 I wasn't sleeping when my parents _____ (come) home last night.

6 **Put the words in the correct order to make sentences.**

1 ? / make / the baby / while / lunch / sleeping / was / Mum / did
   Did Mum make lunch while the baby was sleeping?

2 arrived / was / Joan / sitting / when / the guests / in the garden
   _____

3 ? / Jessica / fall down / she / did / skiing / while / was
   _____

4 we / while / fell asleep / were / watching / we / TV
   _____

5 were / they / playing / Dad / home / when / chess / came
   _____

6 ? / you / waiting / saw / her / were / for / the bus / when / you
   _____

Lesson 3

Vocabulary

1 Complete the dialogues with these words.

become   download   exercise   ~~finish~~   make   stand

1 **A:** What do you do in the afternoons?
   B: When I _____*finish*_____ my homework, I read comics or surf the Internet.

2 **A:** Do you like football or basketball?
   B: I like football, but I can't _____ basketball.

3 **A:** Why do you like surfing?
   B: It's exciting and it's very good _____ too.

4 **A:** How can I _____ songs from the Internet?
   B: It's easy! I'll show you.

5 **A:** Do you have a lot of free time?
   B: Not really, but I always _____ time for my dance lessons!

6 **A:** When did you _____ interested in boxing, Sam?
   B: I started boxing when I was eight!

Grammar

2 Circle the correct words.

1 Anna used / use to listen to music for about two hours every day.
2 Did you used / use to watch music shows on TV?
3 Anna used to playing / play tennis twice a week.
4 'Did you use to download music?' 'Yes, I did / used.'
5 She didn't used / use to have a lot of homework.
6 'Did Peter use to have riding lessons twice a week?' 'No, he didn't / hadn't.'

Express yourself!

3 Complete the dialogue with these sentences.

Do you like painting?   I can't stand doing homework.   Well, I have more time at the weekends.
When did you start cycling?   ~~Tell me about your free time.~~

Interviewer: Emma, you're fourteen and you live in London. **(1)** __*Tell me about your free time.*__

Emma: Well, I haven't got a lot of free time because we get a lot of homework at our school.
(2) _____ It's so boring!

Interviewer: What about your hobbies? **(3)** _____

Emma: No, I hate drawing and painting. I'm not very good at art.

Interviewer: What do you do at the weekends?

Emma: **(4)** _____ I usually go cycling.

Interviewer: **(5)** _____

Emma: I started cycling when I was ten.

Interviewer: Thank you, Emma. And now let's talk to Anna. She's fifteen and …

Writing

4 Complete the story with and, when, or while.

The Accident

Last week, I was walking to the swimming pool with my friends **(1)** _____*and*_____ we were talking about our summer holidays. My best friend David told us about his holiday in Portugal last year.

One day, he was sitting on the beach **(2)** _____ some Portuguese children arrived. They were playing in the water **(3)** _____ they were having fun. Then, one of the boys dived into the water **(4)** _____ a small fishing boat was passing. David's dad dived into the water and he pulled the boy out. He was OK, but he was very scared.

Later that day, the boy spoke to David's dad **(5)** _____ he was reading his book on the beach. He thanked him and he told him his name was Ramirez. He became good friends with David and they spent the rest of their summer holidays together.

Remember!

We use Past Continuous + Past Continuous to set the scene for a story. We use and to join the two parts of the sentence.
The children were playing a board game and their parents were watching television.

We can use Past Simple + Past Continuous to talk about things that happen in a story. We use when before the Past Simple and while before the Past Continuous.
I was dancing at the party when I fell.
I fell while I was dancing at the party.

5 Write a story about an accident. Use this plan to help you.

Paragraph 1
Set the scene. Say when and where the accident happened.

Paragraph 2
Say something about the accident.

Paragraph 3
Say what happened after the accident.

_____
_____
_____
_____
_____
_____
_____
_____
_____
_____

Lesson 1

Vocabulary

1 **Look at the pictures and write the missing letters.**

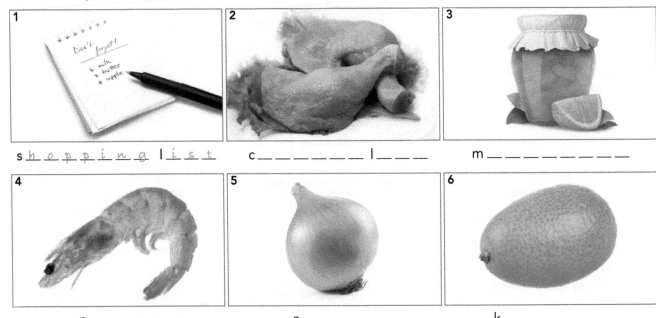

1 s h o p p i n g l i s t

2 c _ _ _ _ _ _ _ l _ _ _ _

3 m _ _ _ _ _ _ _ _ _

4 p _ _ _ _

5 o _ _ _ _

6 k _ _ _ _ _ _ _

2 **Complete the crossword puzzle.**

Across

2 I had ice cream with _____exotic_____ fruit for dessert.

6 That food smells awful. It's _____.

Down

1 This chicken tastes great. It's _____.

3 I didn't have breakfast or lunch. I'm _____!

4 I really need something to drink. I'm _____.

5 I can't eat another piece of pizza. I'm _____.

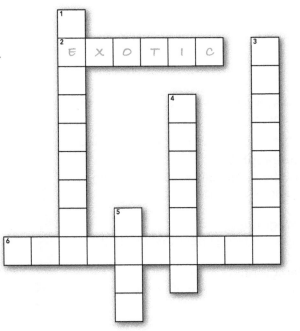

3 **Complete the sentences with these words.**

| dinner juice list noodles recipe site |

1 You can read about exotic fruit on this _____site_____.

2 Can you give me your _____ for tomato soup?

3 How much lemon _____ have we got in the fridge?

4 Kristie wants to cook a surprise birthday _____ for her mum.

5 I can't eat these _____. They taste horrible.

6 Can you please put apples and milk on the shopping _____?

Grammar

4 Complete the sentences with much, many, how much **or** how many.

1 We haven't got _____*many*_____ oranges. There are only two.
2 _____ bananas are there in the basket?
3 '_____ is that cake?' 'Five euros.'
4 There isn't _____ water in this bottle.
5 _____ eggs do we need?
6 There aren't _____ hot dogs on the plate.
7 We can't do it now. We haven't got _____ time.
8 _____ money did he spend?

5 Look at the pictures and write T **(true) or** F **(false).**

1 There are a lot of children at the party. ☐ T
2 There are a few eggs in the bowl. ☐
3 He's got lots of milk. ☐
4 There are only a few oranges. ☐
5 She made a lot of pancakes. ☐
6 She's only got a little orange juice. ☐

6 Match.

1 We haven't got much   a are the eggs?
2 How much   b all together?
3 Grant had a   c chips.
4 How much is it   d lot of bread for breakfast.
5 You can't have many   e cheese. Let's buy some.
6 Can I eat a   f few biscuits?

4 Lesson 2

Vocabulary

1 Match.

1. I can't drink this because it's
2. The Aztecs used cocoa beans
3. It's OK to eat
4. For some people, running water is
5. Montezuma thought chocolate brought
6. When I eat chocolate, I feel

a. him power.
b. a small bar of dark chocolate.
c. a luxury.
d. bitter.
e. happy and relaxed. I love it!
f. to pay for things.

2 Find six food-related words and use them to complete the sentences.

```
X C Q X A F G T V C Q
V Z H A D D W O J Y R
M P J P L B W K S G U
I W O K A L Q T G S D
X R W K R W B H O V E
M T U P A G O G N N D
V Z V V L A I C W L M
W X I Y R Q L H Y I S
U K Q Y H L L O K H E
O S N O A J S P F R Y
J J S L I C E E X Z V
```

1. _____Chop_____ the onions into small pieces.
2. _____ the cheese to the spaghetti.
3. _____ the chicken in hot water for thirty minutes.
4. _____ the prawns in the oil.
5. _____ the sugar, vanilla and milk together.
6. _____ the cake and give everyone a piece.

3 Complete the paragraph with these words.

bar   bitter   calm   cinnamon   luxury

Did you know?

- Eating chocolate makes you feel **(1)** _____calm_____ and relaxed.
- You can mix chocolate with **(2)** _____. You can also mix chocolate with pepper, chilli, tomatoes and meat!
- In 1842, Cadbury's in England created the world's first chocolate **(3)** _____.
- Chocolate isn't a **(4)** _____ anymore, but some kinds of chocolate can be quite expensive. The most expensive chocolate in the world costs €5,000 a kilo.
- **(5)** _____ chocolate or dark chocolate is a lot healthier than milk chocolate.

Grammar

4 Circle the correct words.

1 Here are **some** / any pancakes for you.
2 **Every** / Any child will get a present after the party.
3 Are there **any** / some biscuits in that packet?
4 There is any / **no** sugar in my tea.
5 I went to **every** / any shop in town, but I couldn't find kumquats!
6 There aren't some / **any** restaurants open today.
7 Oh no! There are any / **no** vegetables in the fridge.
8 We need **some** / any butter for the cake.

5 Look at the pictures and complete the sentences with these words.

anywhere everywhere nobody nothing somebody something

Kelly looked _____everywhere_____ for her keys.

There's _____ for lunch!

Matt isn't going _____ tonight because he's tired.

Samantha is putting _____ in her coffee.

There's _____ at the door.

_____ is shopping at the moment.

6 Complete the sentences with these words.

any anything everybody everything no nothing some someone

1 There's _____someone_____ on the phone for you.
2 Have we got _____ juice?
3 Don't worry! I've got _____ money!
4 There's _____ for dinner. Let's go out.
5 I really enjoyed the party. _____ was fantastic.
6 I can't eat _____ at the moment. I'm full.
7 There is _____ milk in the fridge. Please buy some.
8 _____ is here. Let's start!

Lesson 3

Vocabulary

1 Complete the paragraph with these words.

address   cooking   delicious   email   exotic
recipe   ~~webpage~~

○ ○ ○   **Email**

📝 New   ✉ Reply   📋 Forward   🖨 Print   🗑 Delete   ✉ Send & Re

Hi! I'm Whitney and this is my **(1)** _____webpage_____!
I've got lots of friends from around the world and
I **(2)** _____ them all the time. I am mad
about **(3)** _____! My friend Ann sent me
a(n) **(4)** _____ for crocodile curry! It sounds
(5) _____! Have your got any recipes
for **(6)** _____ food? Send them to me
and I will put them on my webpage! My email
(7) _____ is Whitney@ssite.co.uk.

Express yourself!

2 Complete the dialogue with these words or phrases.

a good idea   ~~for dinner~~   I'd like   what
would you

Tina: What's **(1)** _____for dinner_____,
Mum?

Mum: How about making a cheese omellete?

Tina: No, thanks! **(2)** _____ spaghetti.

Mum: But we had spaghetti yesterday.

Tina: That's true.

Mum: **(3)** _____ like a pizza.

Tina: Yes, that's **(4)** _____. I love pizza!

Mum: **(5)** _____ about some ice cream for dessert?

Tina: Sounds great!

Speaking

3 Complete the list about yourself. Use a tick (✓) or a cross (✗).

	like …	don't like …
sandwiches		
chips		
spaghetti		
chocolate		
vegetables		
chicken		
pizza		
prawns		

4 Tell your partner about the food that you like and don't like. Use these words to help you.

awful   delicious   disgusting   tasty

Writing

5 The words/phrases in bold are wrong. Write the correct words/phrases.

Dear Kristen
(1) Love from Monica,

Hi! **(2) Bye for now!** I'm fine. I want to tell you about a delicious meal I had last night.

We went to a new Chinese restaurant in the city. The food was really exotic. **(3) Then**, we had fried prawns. They were amazing. **(4) Last of all**, we had noodles with spicy chicken and vegetables. It was a bit hot, but very tasty! **(5) First**, we had fried bananas with vanilla ice cream for dessert. You must try it. I know you really like ice cream. Let's go to the restaurant together one day.

(6) How are you?

(7) Dear Kristen

Remember!

We begin letters and emails with Dear … and then How are you?

We use First, Then and Last of all to put our ideas in order in the letter or email. This makes it easier for the reader to follow.

We can finish with Bye for now! and Love from … .

6 Write an email to a friend about a disgusting meal. Use this plan to help you.

Begin like this:
Dear _____ (your friend's name),

Answer the questions:
Where did you have the meal?
What did you eat first?
What did you have then?
What was the food like?
Must your friend have a meal there?

End like this:
Bye for now!
Love from _____ (your name)

Reading

1 Read the text about snorkelling.

Do you prefer surfing the waves to surfing the Internet? **(1)** _b_ Then, get yourself a snorkel and a diving mask and go snorkelling! Snorkelling is swimming underwater using a snorkel and it's an exciting activity.

Snorkelling is very popular for a number of reasons. **(2)** ___ The only thing you need to know is how to swim and how to breathe through the snorkel. For safety reasons, however, you shouldn't go snorkelling on your own. **(3)** ___

You can go snorkelling anywhere, but the best places are reefs with warm waters and interesting things to see. **(4)** ___ It's got over 1,500 different kinds of fish, beautiful corals and sponges. The Great Barrier Reef is one of the seven natural wonders of the world.

2 Complete the text with these sentences.

a It's always better to go snorkelling with someone who has got some experience.

b Are you adventurous and good at water sports?

c The Great Barrier Reef in the Coral Sea near Australia is an ideal place for snorkellers.

d You don't need a lot of training or expensive equipment.

Vocabulary

3 **Choose the correct answers.**

1 I'm really sorry – it was all my ___.
   a activity
   (b) fault
   c power

2 ___ the eggs for five minutes and then leave them to cool.
   a Mix
   b Add
   c Boil

3 Mum! Dad! I won the ice-skating ___!
   a competition
   b hobby
   c exercise

4 My brother collects coins. I want to ___ a hobby too.
   a take up
   b go off
   c keep on

5 She used to be mad about cooking, but then she ___.
   a gave it up
   b tried it out
   c kept it on

6 Snowshoeing is ___, but it is tiring too.
   a entertaining
   b boring
   c excited

7 A(n) ___ is a vegetable, not a fruit.
   a prawn
   b onion
   c orange

8 I always make a ___ with the things I need before I go to the supermarket.
   a recipe
   b list
   c bar

9 I had three slices of pizza. I'm ___!
   a starving
   b bitter
   c full

10 He can't waterski well. He needs to ___ more.
   a slide
   b practise
   c step

11 I can't eat this cake. It's too ___ for me.
   a bitter
   b spicy
   c sweet

12 Did you see that skater's tricks? She was ___!
   a relaxing
   b nervous
   c brilliant

Grammar

4 **Choose the correct answers.**

1 Was he climbing up the hill when he ___ down?
   (a) fell
   b was falling
   c falling

2 'Was Patty making dinner when you left?' 'No, ___.'
   a she doesn't
   b she wasn't
   c she didn't

3 Jason didn't ___ like swimming.
   a used to
   b use to
   c use

4 What was Tim doing from six o'clock ___ eight?
   a by
   b at
   c till

5 'Did she use to live in Canada?' 'Yes, she ___.'
   a used
   b did
   c use

6 ___ dinner at 8 o'clock last night?
   a Were you having
   b Do you have
   c You were having

7 There are only ___ eggs in the fridge.
   a a little
   b not much
   c a few

8 There aren't ___ kumquats on the table.
   a some
   b any
   c no

9 I heard a strange noise while I ___ TV.
   a was watching
   b watched
   c watching

10 She had no job and ___ to live.
   a somewhere
   b anywhere
   c nowhere

11 ___ child in my class loves skating.
   a Every
   b Some
   c Any

12 Is there ___ for lunch? We're starving.
   a something
   b anything
   c nothing

Vocabulary

1 **Label the pictures with these words.**

> bell   canteen   cheat   dinosaur   rucksack   sharp teeth

canteen

_____

_____

_____

_____

_____

2 **The words in bold are in the wrong sentences. Write the correct words.**

1 The tyrannosaurus **flashed** 65 million years ago!   ___died out___

2 This museum is **real**! There are so many exhibits!   _____

3 They used the globe and **showed** back in time.   _____

4 Something has just **travelled** in your bag. What is it?   _____

5 Children believe that Santa Claus is a **gigantic** person.   _____

6 The teacher **died out** some fantastic things to the students.   _____

3 **Complete the dialogues with these words.**

> break time   canteen   head teacher   rucksack   term   uniform

1 **A:** What do you usually do at ___break time___?
   B: We play basketball or football.

2 **A:** How long is a school _____ in Greece, Petros?
   B: Three months.

3 **A:** I hate wearing a school _____!
   B: Why? I think it's cool, and you don't have to decide what to wear every morning!

4 **A:** Is that your English teacher?
   B: No, that's our _____, Ms Barnes.

5 **A:** I can't find my MP3 player!
   B: Have you looked in your _____?

6 **A:** I never eat in the school _____ – the food is awful!
   B: I know! I always bring sandwiches from home.

Grammar

4 Complete the paragraph with the Present Perfect Simple of the verbs in brackets.

The students at our school **(1)** ___have been___ (be) very excited this week. It's nearly the end of term and we **(2)** _____ (study) a lot, so now we are having a party. The head teacher **(3)** _____ (help) us a lot. He **(4)** _____ (tell) us that we can use the canteen for drinks and snacks. We **(5)** _____ (already/buy) lots of balloons and we **(6)** _____ (send) the invitations to all the students and teachers. Now, we are just waiting for the big day!

5 Complete the sentences with for, since, already, just or never. **Sometimes more than one answer is possible.**

1 I've been a student in this school ___for___ five years.
2 She's tired because she has _____ had a test.
3 We haven't been to the beach _____ last summer.
4 The term has _____ finished, so we're going on holiday this weekend.
5 Don't send Bill an invitation to the party. I've _____ sent him one.
6 Warren always studies and he has _____ cheated in a test.
7 I've had this laptop _____ a year.
8 I don't want to go to the zoo. I have _____ been there twice this term.

6 Look at the pictures and complete the sentences with these verbs. Use the Present Perfect Simple.

break   buy   draw   make   ~~open~~   wash

He ___has___ just ___opened___ the door.

She _____ the dishes.

Melissa _____ a picture of a house.

They _____ a new house.

Alex _____ his arm.

We _____ just _____ some biscuits!

35

Vocabulary

1 **Write the missing letters.**

1 This is like a test.
e _x_ _a_ _m_

2 You get this when you go to school.
e _ _ _ _ _ _ _ _

3 There are lots of books in here.
l _ _ _ _ _ _

4 Your teacher gives you this at the end of each term.
r _ _ _ _ _ _

5 You have this after you have worked for a long time.
e _ _ _ _ _ _ _ _ _ _

6 You get these for a test.
m _ _ _ _ _

2 **Write S (Subject), PE (Person) or PL (Place).**

1	teacher	PE	**5** champion	
2	lab		**6** coach	
3	science		**7** gym	
4	skate park		**8** music	

3 **Circle the correct words.**

1 Four students have won Olympic medals / marks.

2 The school has been very successful / normal since it opened in 1972.

3 He trains hard and wants to become a staff / champion one day.

4 Get your bike – we're going snowboarding / cycling!

5 I've just come back from the gym / theatre. I love exercising!

6 Our school has got a computer lab and two indoor / professional swimming pools.

7 We are looking for a basketball coach with a lot of experience / education.

Grammar

4 **Complete the sentences with** ever **or** yet**.**

1 I haven't been to the library _____yet_____.
2 Has she _____ cheated in a test?
3 They haven't taken their reports _____.
4 The game hasn't finished _____.
5 Has the coach _____ shouted at you?
6 Have you _____ finished your homework before 8 o'clock?

5 **Choose the correct answers.**

1 He hasn't ___ me the email yet.
  a send
  b sending
  c sent ⟵

2 'Have you been to the new sports centre?'
'No, ___.'
  a I have
  b I haven't
  c haven't I

3 Have you ___ seen a real elephant?
  a ever
  b yet
  c never

4 Has he finished his science project ___?
  a since
  b yet
  c ever

5 The school term ___ yet.
  a has started
  b hasn't started
  c has never started

6 'Have they ever won medals?' 'Yes, they ___.'
  a won
  b did
  c have

6 **Look at the pictures and write questions and short answers with the Present Perfect Simple.**

? / they / go to the zoo
Have they gone to the zoo?
No, they haven't.
_____

? / Jennifer / open her present
_____
_____
_____

? / Mark / buy a new car
_____
_____
_____

? / Ashley / make biscuits
_____
_____
_____

? / Kevin / finish the exam / yet
_____
_____
_____

? / the boys / win medals
_____
_____
_____

Vocabulary

1 Circle the correct words.

1 I saw the advert / magazine for the job on the Internet.
2 Has your teacher moved / given you lots of homework?
3 She gets on / gets off very well with everybody.
4 The reporter has interviewed / taught our science teacher.
5 'What do you think of the teaching people / staff?' 'I think they're great!'

Express yourself!

2 Complete the dialogue with these questions.

What are you bad at?   What are you good at?   What is your favourite subject?
Where do you go to school?   Who is your favourite teacher?

Jason: Hi Sue, this is my friend Ian. He goes to my school.

Sue: Hi Ian.

Ian: Hi! Yes, Jason and I have been classmates for four years now.
(1) _Where do you go to school?_

Sue: I go to school in Bath.

Ian: (2) _____

Sue: My favourite subject is science. What about you?

Ian: I like geography. I'm bad at science.

Sue: Really? (3) _____

Ian: I'm very good at history.

Sue: Me too!

Ian: (4) _____

Sue: I'm bad at art. I don't like drawing and making things. And I don't get on with my art teacher, Ms Pane.

Ian: (5) _____

Sue: My favourite teacher is Mr Cole. He always takes us to cool places like museums and the theatre.

Grammar

3 Look at the pictures and complete the questions with How long and the Present Perfect Simple of these verbs.

be   have   live   play   teach   work

1 ___How long has___ Thomas ___been___ in the library?

2 _____ Ashley _____ the drums?

3 _____ Emily _____ in this office?

4 _____ Mr Evans _____ maths?

5 _____ the Thomsons _____ in this house?

6 _____ Ethan _____ a pet hamster?

Writing

4 Complete the email describing an English language school with these topic sentences.

I go to the Simple English Language School in Athens.

The thing I like best is writing.

The school has a staff of four teachers.

There is only one thing I don't like about the language school.

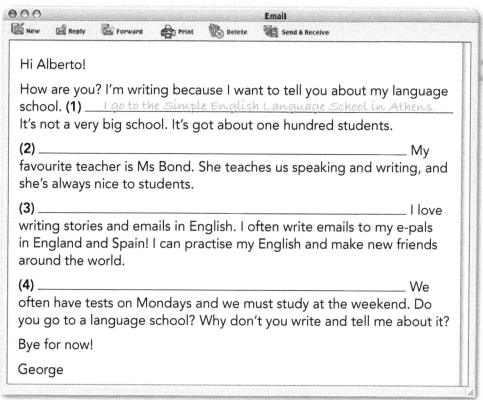

○○○   **Email**

New   Reply   Forward   Print   Delete   Send & Receive

Hi Alberto!

How are you? I'm writing because I want to tell you about my language school. **(1)** _I go to the Simple English Language School in Athens._ It's not a very big school. It's got about one hundred students.

(2) _____ My favourite teacher is Ms Bond. She teaches us speaking and writing, and she's always nice to students.

(3) _____ I love writing stories and emails in English. I often write emails to my e-pals in England and Spain! I can practise my English and make new friends around the world.

(4) _____ We often have tests on Mondays and we must study at the weekend. Do you go to a language school? Why don't you write and tell me about it?

Bye for now!

George

5 Write an email to a friend describing your English language school. Use this plan to help you.

Paragraph 1
Say what English language school you go to and where it is. Say how big the school is.

Paragraph 2
Say something about the teachers. Talk about your favourite teacher.

Paragraph 3
Say something about what you like best. Say why you like it.

Paragraph 4
Say something you don't like about your English language school. End your email.

Vocabulary

1 **Complete the dialogue with these words.**

abroad   bodies   colourful   documentary   paint   tribe

Phil: Hi Ginny! I watched a very interesting **(1)** ___documentary___ called *Our World* last night!

Ginny: I watched it too!

Phil: Wasn't that African **(2)** _____ amazing?

Ginny: Yes, I really liked their costumes and their **(3)** _____ necklaces.

Phil: And both men and women in that tribe **(4)** _____ their faces.

Ginny: Yes, their faces and their **(5)** _____ too!

Phil: I've always wanted to travel **(6)** _____. Now I know where I want to go – Africa!

2 **Find eight body-related words and use them to complete the sentences.**

U	L	I	S	S	C	H	E	S	T	H	R
D	I	B	B	T	H	R	O	A	T	Y	R
Y	E	L	B	O	W	S	U	K	O	B	P
W	T	A	G	M	Q	E	T	D	K	G	D
V	K	B	H	A	N	K	L	E	N	V	K
D	P	X	N	C	M	U	K	H	E	Z	O
G	Z	N	S	H	O	U	L	D	E	R	I
H	O	Y	S	R	Q	O	R	Y	U	V	Z
N	A	V	F	S	J	P	F	D	A	E	H
Y	J	I	I	T	A	I	L	W	O	J	G

1 I've eaten too much pizza and my ___stomach___ hurts.

2 Your _____ is at the top of your arm.

3 My _____ is between my foot and my leg.

4 It's rude to put your _____ on the table when you eat.

5 My _____ is in the middle of my leg.

6 I don't have a(n) _____ but my cat, Sweetie, does!

7 I can't speak – my _____ hurts.

8 The part of your body between your neck and your stomach is your _____.

3 **Match.**

1 The albatross has landed

2 My dog has got

3 I've never travelled

4 He looked

5 In this tribe men paint

6 She was wearing

a so handsome in his uniform!

b their chests and arms.

c on the water.

d a black and white tail.

e abroad.

f a beautiful necklace.

Grammar

4 **Complete the sentences with the Past Simple or the Present Perfect Simple of these verbs.**

cut have land live not tidy travel ~~wash~~

1 Karen _____has washed_____ her hair twice today.
2 Lydia _____ her bedroom and it's messy.
3 My younger brother _____ his hand with a knife last night.
4 Mikey and Kristie _____ abroad lots of times.
5 We _____ breakfast and then we got ready for school.
6 Look! The bird _____ on a rock in the sea.
7 They _____ in London many years ago.

5 **Match.**

1 I broke my ankle
2 When I was at school,
3 Stan hasn't seen Irene
4 They haven't been at work for a month,
5 He has never
6 We sat down, turned on the TV

a and watched a documentary.
b I always got bad marks.
c so they haven't got any money.
d since 1999.
e last week.
f travelled by plane.

6 **Answer the questions.**

1 Have you ever broken your ankle? _____
2 Did you brush your hair this morning? _____
3 Did your stomach hurt last night? _____
4 Have you just got up? _____
5 Has your best friend ever stayed at your house? _____
6 Did your parents have pets when they were young? _____
7 Did you go to the cinema last weekend? _____
8 Has the head teacher ever shouted at you? _____

Vocabulary

1 The words in bold are in the wrong sentences. Write the correct words.

1 I've got a terrible **war** in my chest. _____pain_____
2 Chinese people think that the colour red brings good **make-up**. _____
3 Some people in Africa **scare** animals for food. _____
4 Does your mother often wear **luck** at work? _____
5 Stop that noise. You'll **hunt** the baby! _____
6 They always paint their bodies red when they go to **pain**. _____

2 Complete the dialogues with these words.

burn headache skin temperature throat toothache

1 A: How does this tribe make clothes?
   B: They make them from the _____skin_____ of animals.

2 A: Are you OK? Why are holding your head?
   B: I've got a terrible _____!

3 A: The baby is very hot.
   B: Oh no. Do you think he's got a _____?

4 A: Why has she gone to the dentist?
   B: She had a _____.

5 A: Would you like some ice cream for dessert?
   B: No, thank you. I've got a sore _____.

6 A: Tony, there's a _____ on your hand!
   B: Yes, I wasn't careful and the oven was hot!

3 Complete the paragraph with these words.

actors face painting make-up scare tribe war

Body Painting Facts

People around the world have used body painting for a number of reasons.

- Tribes in America painted their faces red or black when they went to (1) _____war_____. Different tribes painted their faces and bodies in different ways. Each tribe had its own way of (2) _____ for special days.

- Women in ancient Egypt were the first to wear (3) _____. They painted their eyes black to look more beautiful.

- In Chinese theatre (4) _____ painted their faces red, white or black. Face make-up was much better than wearing masks.

- Men and women of the Maasai (5) _____ paint their bodies and faces. Maasai men often spend hours or days decorating their bodies. They believe that their body paint will (6) _____ their enemies.

42

Grammar

4 **Complete the sentences with possessive pronouns.**

1 Please give this necklace to Joanna. It's _____hers_____. (her)
2 'Whose car do you like better?' 'I like _____.' (his)
3 That MP3 player isn't _____. (your)
4 'These pictures are beautiful.' 'Thank you, they are _____.' (our)
5 'My head hurts.' 'So does _____.' (my)
6 He's not our maths teacher. He's _____. (their)

5 **Choose the correct answers.**

1 'Can I use this laptop?' 'No, it's not ___.
  a my
  ⓑ mine
  c our

2 I found this MP3 player under Tim's desk.
  Is it ___?
  a him
  b he
  c his

3 Those are ___ keys on the table, not Kelly's.
  a ours
  b us
  c our

4 'My feet are cold.' 'So ___.'
  a are mine
  b do mine
  c mine are

5 That's Kristie and Mikey's magic globe.
  It's ___.
  a them
  b their
  c theirs

6 Is that ___ rucksack or yours?
  a hers
  b her
  c she

6 **Complete the sentences with** mine, yours, his, hers, ours **or** theirs.

1 Give Adam his ice-skates. They are
  _____his_____.
2 These DVDs aren't _____. We haven't got any DVDs.
3 Helen, are those trainers _____?
4 'Is this your mobile phone or Julia's?' 'It isn't mine, it's _____.'
5 I want my skateboard back. It's _____!
6 'Are these Mum and Dad's keys?' 'Yes, they're _____.'

Vocabulary

1 **Match.**

1 I played computer games and then I surfed the Internet for hours.

2 I don't want to stay up late.

3 I've eaten a lot of pizza.

4 I carry a very heavy rucksack.

5 I walked home from work.

6 I fell down the stairs.

a My stomach hurts.

b I've broken my arm.

c My feet are sore.

d I've got a terrible headache.

e My back is sore.

f I want a good night's sleep.

Express yourself!

2 **Complete the dialogue with these sentences.**

I've got a bad cough.   Is it serious?   Open your mouth.   Take this medicine.   What's the matter?

Ryan: I feel awful!

Doctor: **(1)** _What's the matter?_____

Ryan: **(2)** _____ I've had it for a week now.

Doctor: **(3)** _____

Ryan: Well? **(4)** _____

Doctor: No, it isn't. **(5)** _____ You'll be fine in a few days.

Ryan: Thank you, Doctor.

Speaking

3 **Circle the words that relate to health problems.**

1 (cough)

2 tribe

3 toothache

4 spots

5 reason

6 pain

7 temperature

8 advice

9 sore

10 headache

11 throat

12 sneeze

13 skin

14 ankle

4 **Tell your partner about a health problem you have had. Use the words that you circled in 3.**

Writing

5 **Read the letter below and put the paragraphs in the correct order.**

Hi Owen,

☐ I've been sick for about ten days now. Mum was a bit scared, so she took me to the doctor's this morning. Do you remember Dr Bones? He's grown old, but he's still there! He said, 'Open your mouth.' He looked inside and said, 'This doesn't look good!'

☐ Well, now I'm at home and resting as the doctor said. Why don't you come to see me at the weekend? You can tell me all your news then.

☒ How are you? I'm really sick at the moment. I'm not at school, so I've got time for a short email. I've got a horrible cold and a really sore throat.

☐ After that, he had a good look in my ears. He said, 'I can't see anything wrong with your ears.' Mum thinks he can't see at all! Then he said to Mum, 'Don't worry, she's just got a sore throat. She needs to take this medicine every morning for a week. She can't get cold and she needs to stay in bed for a couple of days.' So, we came back home.

See you soon,

Melanie

Remember!

There are three parts in a piece of writing: the beginning, the middle and the end. The beginning introduces the subject. The middle gives details. The end finishes the piece of writing.

6 **Write a letter to a friend about your doctor or dentist. Use this plan to help you.**

Begin like this:
Hi _____ (your friend's name),

Paragraph 1
Say why you are writing. Introduce your doctor or dentist and say a few things about him/her.

Paragraphs 2 and 3
Talk about a visit to your doctor or your dentist. Say what happened and what he/she was like.

Paragraph 4
Say goodbye to your friend and arrange to meet soon.

Finish like this:
See you soon!
_____ (your name)

Reading

1 Read the text about a specialist music school.

Learning is an art, and all students are artists. This is true for the students in Purcell School in Bushey, UK, a special music school for children and Britain's oldest specialist school.

At Purcell School, students have normal classes in English, maths and science, but they also have music lessons. After their classes, they practise music for three to six hours every day! There are daily concerts at lunch time and evening concerts with the school orchestra and visiting musicians. The school has organised music tours and has given concerts in countries like Japan, Germany and Russia!

Purcell School has been very successful since it opened in 1962. In 2003, it won the UNESCO Mozart Medal for its contribution to music and education. Its students have won competitions and become professional musicians. Daisy Chute, the *All Angels* singer, was a Purcell student and Alex Ullman, another Purcell student, won the International Piano Competition in Budapest in 2011.

If you have a passion for music, you can audition and become a student at Purcell School! Apply now and make your dream come true!

2 Circle the correct words.

1 Purcell School is the oldest specialist school / oldest school in the UK.

2 Students at Purcell School practise music for up to six hours every week / day.

3 Students have given concerts only in the UK / in countries around the world.

4 The school won a medal in 1962 / 2003.

5 Daisy Chute / Alex Ullman is a singer.

Vocabulary

3 Choose the correct answers.

1 How long has Mr Smith been the head ___ at your school?
  a teacher
  b champion
  c coach

2 Have you seen the ___ about people in Africa?
  a wedding
  b documentary
  c war

3 He's talented and he will be very ___ as a photographer.
  a gigantic
  b successful
  c real

4 My mother has had this ___ since she was twenty.
  a necklace
  b tribe
  c tail

5 Your ___ is in the middle of your leg.
  a ankle
  b knee
  c elbow

6 Samantha had an awful ___, so she went to the dentist.
  a headache
  b burn
  c toothache

7 'There's a red light over there and it's ___.' 'What can it be?'
  a flashing
  b dying out
  c showing

8 He's got a lovely face. He's very ___.
  a handsome
  b common
  c colourful

9 The school has got a computer ___ and an indoor swimming pool.
  a gym
  b park
  c lab

10 Oh no! My kite has ___ on the roof of that house!
  a landed
  b scared
  c hunted

11 How many ___ are there in a school year?
  a medals
  b terms
  c reports

12 Emily had a good ___ ; I'm sure she will do well in life.
  a experience
  b university
  c education

Grammar

4 Choose the correct answers.

1 The school bell has just ___.
  a ring
  b rung
  c rang

2 'Have they painted the sitting room yet?' 'No, they ___.'
  a haven't
  b weren't
  c didn't

3 I've ___ here before!
  a be
  b was
  c been

4 She's been a teacher in this school ___ five years now.
  a since
  b already
  c for

5 I've ___ taken my medicine. It was very bitter.
  a never
  b just
  c since

6 ___ to the gym yesterday?
  a Have you gone
  b Did you go
  c You went

7 How long ___ this cough?
  a you have had
  b have you had
  c you have

8 When he was young, he ___ a necklace from a shop.
  a has stolen
  b stole
  c stolen

9 ___ you spoken to the doctor yet?
  a Did
  b Has
  c Have

10 'Our teacher always shouts at us.' '___ doesn't.'
  a Our
  b Ours
  c Us

11 Please give this report to Sandy. It's ___.
  a hers
  b her
  c she

12 'My arms are sore.' 'So are ___.'
  a me
  b my
  c mine

Vocabulary

1 Match.

1 Hurry up! We don't want to miss
2 Put some sun cream on or your face
3 I'm sure she'll be here
4 Don't go. I don't want to be
5 Oh no! I forgot

a in a second.
b our favourite TV programme!
c on my own.
d all about his visit!
e will go red.

2 Complete the crossword.

Across

1 This is part of a tree with leaves or fruit on it.
3 This is the top part of the earth where plants grow.
5 This is a large area of land where people grow things.
6 These are small pieces of rock that we find on the ground.

Down

2 Birds lay their eggs and live in this.
4 These grow on trees and they turn yellow in autumn.

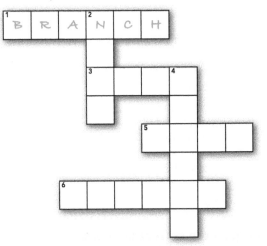

3 Complete the dialogues with these words.

environment frilled natural nest recorder second

1 A: Where do lizards live?
   B: They live all over the world, but _____frilled_____ lizards live in Australia.

2 A: Look! There is a(n) _____ in that tree!
   B: Do you think there are any eggs in it?

3 A: There is a really good documentary on TV at 3 o'clock.
   B: We can turn on the DVD _____ and watch it when we get back.

4 A: What kind of _____ do polar bears live in?
   B: Cold and wet.

5 A: What do you like about this office?
   B: It's got a lot of _____ light.

6 A: It's getting late. We have to go.
   B: I'll be ready in a(n) _____.

Grammar

4 Complete the sentences with these verbs. Use the Future Simple or be going to.

be   feed   not forget   not snow   wear   work

1 Susan _____is going to be_____ away for two days next week. She told me last night.
2 I can't believe you _____ your red dress again. Haven't you got anything else?
3 I think Phillip _____ this weekend.
4 _____ you _____ the rabbits, please?
5 It _____ tonight – I watched the news on TV.
6 I'm sure she _____ your birthday.

5 Answer the questions.

1 Are you going to the cinema today?
_____

2 Will your class go on a trip next week?
_____

3 Where will you be at 5 o'clock tomorrow?
_____

4 What are you going to do after your English class today?
_____

5 Is your teacher going to give you a test tomorrow?
_____

6 Is it going to rain this afternoon?
_____

7 What are you going to do this Sunday?
_____

6 Look at the pictures and complete the sentences with the Future Simple or be going to.

1 I'm sure you _____will_____ take some nice photos.

2 It _____ rain soon.

3 I think I _____ make something to eat.

4 He's very talented. I'm sure he _____ be famous one day!

5 I _____ help you carry this box. It's very heavy.

6 She _____ go on a trip this Sunday.

Vocabulary

1 Complete the dialogues with these words.

display face hiss neck spot

1 A: Where can I see his new paintings?
   B: They're on _____display_____ in the Museum of Modern Art.

2 A: What's that pink bird with the long _____?
   B: It's a flamingo.

3 A: Do snakes _____?
   B: Yes, when they are afraid.

4 A: Can you _____ Joe?
   B: No, I can't. There are a lot of people in the room.

5 A: What does a frilled lizard do when it has to _____ an enemy?
   B: It opens its mouth wide and runs!

2 Look at the pictures and write the missing letters.

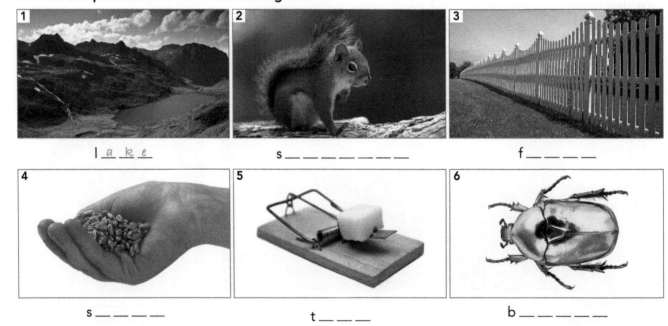

| 1 | 2 | 3 |
| l a k e | s __ __ __ __ __ __ | f __ __ __ __ |

| 4 | 5 | 6 |
| s __ __ __ __ | t __ __ __ | b __ __ __ __ __ |

3 Complete the paragraph with these words.

beetles hiss necks spot wildlife

Fun Facts about Animals

- Ants and **(1)** _____beetles_____ are the most common insects in the world.
- You can't **(2)** _____ lizards easily because they take the colour of their natural environment.
- Flamingos have 17 bones in their **(3)** _____.
- Cats **(4)** _____ when they want to frighten you.
- There are lots of different kinds of **(5)** _____ in Australia. About 100 kinds of marsupials only live in Australia.

Grammar

4 **Complete the sentences with gerunds formed from the verbs in brackets.**

1 I enjoy _____*feeding*_____ (feed) the animals at the zoo.
2 Jason isn't very good at _____ (look after) plants.
3 We miss _____ (walk) in the forest.
4 _____ (live) in the city isn't always easy.
5 I don't remember _____ (swim) in the lake when I was young.
6 My favourite thing is _____ (take) photos of animals.

5 **Look at the pictures and write T (true) or F (false).**

1 Playing in the park is fun. ☐ T
2 Working on a farm is easy. ☐
3 Steve doesn't like getting up early in the morning. ☐
4 Sue hates cleaning her house. ☐
5 Mark is very good at cooking. ☐
6 Walking on ice is easy. ☐

6 **Put the words in the correct order to make sentences.**

1 can't / she / farm / on / working / the / stand
   She can't stand working on the farm.
2 animals / dangerous / feeding / is / wild
   _____
3 misses / her / spending / friends / she / time / with
   _____
4 looking after / very / plants / good / not / at / I'm
   _____
5 in / hate / they / the / helping / garden
   _____
6 in / office / is / working / boring / an
   _____

Vocabulary

1 Circle the correct words.

1 I don't like it when people are warm / **cruel** to animals.
2 People **bring** / **treat** sick animals to the rescue centre.
3 We've got three **vets** / **pets** at home – a squirrel and two goldfish.
4 My dog had a(n) **rescue** / **accident** yesterday. He's got a broken leg.
5 Our hamster was **seriously** / **awfully** ill and we took it to the vet.
6 Most people **treat** / **leave** their pets well and never hurt them.

Express yourself!

2 Complete the dialogue with these words.

cuddly funny fur hutch rabbit sleep

Tim: Tell me about your new pet, Liz.
Liz: Well, it is very **(1)** _____cuddly_____. I want to hold it all day.
           It's really **(2)** _____ too. It makes me laugh.
Tim: Does it **(3)** _____ in a basket?
Liz: No, it doesn't.
Tim: OK, so it isn't a cat.
Liz: No, it isn't a cat. But it's got **(4)** _____ like a cat.
Tim: Does your pet sleep in a **(5)** _____?
Liz: Yes!
Tim: Your pet is a **(6)** _____, isn't it?
Liz: That's right!

Grammar

3 Choose the correct answers.

1 You've got a cute rabbit, ___?
   a haven't you
   b don't you
   c isn't it

2 She's taking the dog to the vet, ___?
   a hasn't she
   b doesn't she
   c isn't she

3 I'm your best friend, ___?
   a am I
   b aren't I
   c haven't I

4 You didn't clean the hutch, ___?
   a could you
   b didn't you
   c did you

5 We can take good care of them, ___?
   a don't we
   b can't we
   c aren't we

6 The squirrel ___ really cute, wasn't it?
   a is
   b wasn't
   c was

7 Ron's pets are very furry, aren't ___?
   a they
   b he
   c it

8 He wasn't seriously ill, ___?
   a will he
   b is he
   c was he

Writing

4 **Read the description of a pet below. Find eight mistakes with punctuation and capital letters and correct them.**

My best friend is my dog. She's called ᴹmaggie and she's six years old. Maggie is very furry and cuddly.

We do everything together. we go for long walks in the park and we watch DVDs together She makes me laugh when I'm sad. She's fantastic?

Maggie loves good food! She likes biscuits meat, rice, vegetables and dog food, but her favourite food is cooked Chicken. Most dogs love eating chicken, don't they!

I love spending time with Maggie. She sleeps on a rug in my bedroom. She wakes me up at 7 o'clock every morning. It's great having a pet dog isn't it?

> **Remember!**
>
> **Punctuation and capital letters**
> We use capital letters to begin:
> * names. *Joanne*
> * places. *Australia*
> * sentences. *She's taking the dog to the vet.*
>
> Sentences end with a full stop, or an exclamation mark for emphasis.
> *The garden looks really nice.*
> *Don't play in the garden!*
>
> Questions end with a question mark.
> *Are you leaving tomorrow?*
>
> We use commas to separate:
> * words in a list. *cats, dogs, lizards and squirrels*
> * question tags from the rest of a sentence. *The cat is sick, isn't it?*

5 **Write a description of your pet or a friend's pet. Use this plan to help you.**

Paragraph 1
Say what kind of pet you or your friend has got. Describe what it looks like.

Paragraph 2
Say what you do or your friend does with the pet.

Paragraph 3
Say what the pet likes.

Paragraph 4
Say how you feel or how your friend feels about the pet and end the description.

Vocabulary

1 Complete the dialogue with these words.

apart   away   electronic   ~~plant~~   protect   separately

Man: Welcome to the electronics recycling **(1)** _____plant_____, children.

Emily: Do you only recycle old TVs and radios? We've got an old washing machine at home. Can you recycle that too?

Man: Sure! We can recycle anything that's **(2)** _____.

Emily: How do you do that?

Man: First, we take it **(3)** _____ and then we recycle each part **(4)** _____.

Emily: Wow! I'll never throw anything **(5)** _____ again!

Man: You see it's not difficult to save energy and **(6)** _____ the environment.

2 Complete the crossword.

Across

1 We carry things in this.

4 We put things that we throw away in this.

5 This gives energy to things like clocks, radios and toys.

6 This means to keep someone or something safe.

Down

1 This is made of glass or plastic and we can recycle it.

2 This is made of aluminium and we put drinks in it.

3 This is something we read.

3 Write G (Glass), PA (Paper) or PL (Plastic).

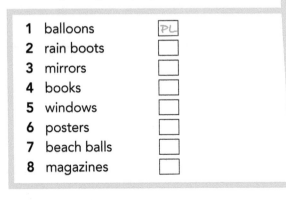

1	balloons	PL
2	rain boots	
3	mirrors	
4	books	
5	windows	
6	posters	
7	beach balls	
8	magazines	

Grammar

4 Look at the pictures and complete the First Conditional sentences with these phrases.

> not die out   not use a lot of water   protect the environment   ~~put litter in the bins~~   recycle them
> use paper bags

If we __put litter in the bins__, the park will be clean.

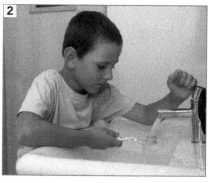

We will help our planet if we _____.

If we clean the beaches, animals _____.

If you collect glass bottles, we _____.

If they _____, they will save energy.

If she recycles newspapers, she _____.

5 Circle the correct words.

1 If we won't / **don't** recycle plastic, the environment will be in danger.
2 More people are coming / **will come** to the park if we clean it.
3 If you take the cans to the recycling plant, I **will help** / help you.
4 If you **don't** / won't throw away your rubbish, your room won't be tidy.
5 We are saving / **will save** energy if we use plastic bags again.
6 If you won't / **don't** need this old oven, we can recycle it.

6 Complete the First Conditional sentences with the verbs in brackets.

Interviewer:	Today, I'm speaking to Rachel Green. She works with Save the Environment Now! Rachel, why do we need to 'save the environment now'?
Rachel:	Well, if we **(1)** ___don't look after___ (not look after) the environment now, we **(2)** _____ (harm) our planet.
Interviewer:	What **(3)** _____ (happen) if we **(4)** _____ (do) that?
Rachel:	Good question. If we **(5)** _____ (not protect) our forests, animals **(6)** _____ (die out). If all animals die out, people **(7)** _____ (be) in great danger too.
Interviewer:	**(8)** _____ (it/help) if we **(9)** _____ (recycle)?
Rachel:	Of course it will. If we recycle, we **(10)** _____ (save) energy and help our planet. We can recycle as much as 80% of our litter!

Vocabulary

1 **Find six environment-related words and use them to complete the sentences.**

Z	P	L	V	Z	G	H	U	R	D	B	Y
P	O	D	V	O	D	D	R	D	H	P	F
A	L	V	O	R	U	G	L	X	O	W	O
E	L	E	C	T	R	I	C	I	T	Y	R
R	U	B	B	I	S	H	L	M	Y	D	L
Z	T	N	F	E	L	B	I	M	T	T	T
A	I	K	F	K	B	A	M	P	N	B	Z
R	O	E	S	S	O	L	A	R	W	Q	Q
U	N	X	O	P	O	K	T	N	Z	A	L
B	M	Y	P	P	A	N	E	L	B	P	O

1 The _____climate_____ in Greece is warm and dry.

2 There will be more air _____ if we go everywhere by car.

3 _____ power is clean and it doesn't harm the environment.

4 Throw away the _____ and tidy your room.

5 A _____ is a flat piece of glass that we put on our roofs.

6 You will pay less for _____ if you turn off the lights when you leave the room.

2 **Complete the sentences with these words.**

> cause   harm   pollute   protect   turn off   ~~waste~~

1 Use a glass of water when you brush your teeth. Don't _____waste_____ water.

2 Too many cars can _____ air pollution.

3 Please _____ the lights when you leave your room.

4 Does air pollution _____ the environment?

5 What can we do to _____ wildlife? I don't want animals to die.

6 If we went everywhere by bike, we wouldn't _____ the air.

3 **Complete the dialogues with these words.**

> climate   electricity   ~~fact~~   forecast   products

1 **A:** Do you recycle glass bottles and cans?
B: Yes. In _____fact_____, I'm going to the recycling plant this afternoon.

2 **A:** What will happen if the _____ changes?
B: Well, the planet will get really hot!

3 **A:** That oven uses a lot of _____.
B: I know. That's why I don't use it every day.

4 **A:** Has anybody heard the weather _____ today?
B: Yes, it's going to rain.

5 **A:** I always buy green _____ that don't harm the environment.
B: Good idea!

Grammar

4 Complete the Second Conditional sentences with the verbs in brackets.

1 If there _____weren't_____ (not be) any recycling bins in my town, I _____would start_____ (start) a recycling group.

2 _____ (you/use) solar power if it _____ (help) the environment?

3 If everyone _____ (turn off) their lights for one hour, we _____ (save) a lot of energy.

4 Our planet _____ (not be) in danger if everyone _____ (go) green.

5 You _____ (not harm) the environment if you _____ (use) plastic bags again and again.

6 If we _____ (recycle) 90% of our waste, _____ (we/protect) our planet?

5 Choose the correct answers.

1 If everyone ___ the beaches, they would be clean.
  a looks after
  b will look after
  c looked after

2 If I ___ you, I'd use paper bags.
  a weren't
  b were
  c would be

3 ___ if I wrote an article about pollution?
  a Would it help
  b Does it help
  c Did it help

4 If she ___ her hair twice a day, she would save water.
  a wouldn't wash
  b didn't wash
  c hasn't washed

5 If they polluted the lake, all the wildlife ___.
  a dies
  b died
  c would die

6 Would your mum shop there if they ___ green products?
  a sell
  b sold
  c are selling

6 Answer the questions with the Second Conditional. Use the words in brackets.

1 What would your parents do if you told them to recycle more? (listen to me)
  If I told my parents to recycle more, they would listen to me.

2 What would you do if you saw people polluting the beach? (shout at them)
  _____

3 What would you do if you worked for an environment group? (write an article)
  _____

4 What would happen if we used things again and again? (not have so much rubbish)
  _____

5 What would you do if you had an old computer? (find an electronics recycling plant)
  _____

6 How would you feel if lions and tigers died out? (not be happy)
  _____

Vocabulary

1 Match.

1 What will happen if we pollute the sea?
2 What's a good way to save energy?
3 What are you going to do with those bottles?
4 What can we recycle?
5 Why must we keep the beach clean?

a Plastic, paper, glass bottles and clothes.
b Animals will die out.
c Because sea turtles make their nests here.
d Using the same bags and bottles again and again.
e I'm going to take them to the recycling bin.

Express yourself!

2 Look at the pictures and complete the sentences with these phrases.

always throw away rubbish   always turn off the lights   never pollute the beach
recycle plastic bottles   ride my bike to work

I ___never pollute the beach___.   I _____.   I _____.

I _____.   I _____.

Speaking

3 Tell your partner about what you do for the environment.

Writing

4 Read the poster and circle the correct words.

Go Green! Help the Planet!

Do you want to help the environment, but you don't know how? Here is what you can do!

Tell people!

Start a green group in your neighbourhood and tell your friends about it. If you told everyone why we must protect the environment, they **(1)** help / **would help** you! If you **(2)** create / **created** a 'green blog', other people would read it and become interested too!

Save energy!

Find the 'green shops' in your neighbourhood! If you **(3)** buy / **bought** green products, you would help the planet. Use less electricity! If you turned off the lights of your bedroom when you went to the living room, you **(4)** **would save** / saved a lot of energy! Simple, isn't it?

Recycle!

Don't throw anything away! If you **(5)** recycled / **would recycle** glass, paper and your old toys and clothes, you would protect our planet! If you recycled one can, you **(6)** **would save** / saved enough energy to power a TV for 3 hours!

> **Remember!**
>
> We can use the Second Conditional to give advice. *If I were you, I wouldn't buy so many plastic products. You would save water if you turned off the tap when you brushed your teeth.*

5 Make a poster about recycling. Use the poster in 4 to help you.

_____

_____

_____

_____

_____

_____

_____

_____

_____

_____

Reading

1 Read the text about sea turtles.

Sea turtles are fascinating creatures. They are reptiles and they have been on earth for 150 million years! We can find sea turtles in all the oceans except the Arctic. Sea turtles can live to be over 80 years old.

Female turtles make their nests on beaches. The females come out of the sea, make holes and then lay their eggs in the soft sand. After 45–70 days, the baby turtles come out of the eggs at night and they head for the sea. Female turtles lay about 100 eggs at a time, but only a few of them, usually one or two, will live to become adult sea turtles.

There are seven kinds of sea turtles and all of them are slowly dying out. Sharks, birds and tourists are to blame. They can harm the nests, the eggs or the baby turtles. In addition, people still hunt and kill them for their meat and eggs. Rubbish on beaches and swimming in polluted ocean water can also harm turtles. Environmental groups around the world are working hard to protect them.

2 Answer the questions.

1 Where can we find sea turtles?
   In all the oceans except the Arctic.

2 Where do female turtles make their nests?
   _____

3 How many kinds of turtles are dying out?
   _____

4 Why do people hunt them?
   _____

5 Who are trying to protect sea turtles?
   _____

Vocabulary

3 Choose the correct answers.

1 If we all recycled, we wouldn't have so much plastic ___.
a soil
b climate
(c) waste

2 Is this the lizard's ___ environment?
a bright
b natural
c frilled

3 ___ your sister in this crowded room won't be easy.
a Facing
b Spotting
c Hissing

4 I need ___ for my clock.
a batteries
b plants
c cans

5 Listen to the ___ on the radio before you go on a picnic.
a litter bin
b solar power
c weather forecast

6 A ___ is a place where birds lay their eggs.
a branch
b farm
c nest

7 Don't ___ that computer. It'll never be the same again!
a take apart
b throw away
c turn off

8 There are so many things you can do to ___ energy.
a save
b protect
c rescue

9 There's a big garden and a wooden ___ round the house.
a pond
b fence
c collar

10 Solar panels turn energy from the sun into ___.
a electricity
b pollution
c environment

11 If you go to Canada in September, you'll see lots of colourful ___ on the trees.
a leaves
b stones
c seeds

12 What kind of a ___ is that thing with six legs?
a creature
b stone
c wildlife

Grammar

4 Choose the correct answers.

1 They're ___ throw away those old clothes tomorrow.
(a) going to
b will
c going

2 ___ take the dog to the vet?
a Is he
b Will he
c Is he going

3 I'm sure the climate ___ in the next hundred years.
a is changing
b changes
c will change

4 I can't stand ___ food.
a to waste
b wasting
c waste

5 ___ plants is not easy.
a To look after
b Look after
c Looking after

6 Clare cares about the environment, ___ she?
a hasn't
b doesn't
c won't

7 We would pay less for electricity if we ___ solar power.
a use
b are using
c used

8 You didn't turn on the DVD recorder, ___?
a did you
b were you
c didn't you

9 If you wanted to protect the environment, what ___?
a do you do
b will you do
c would you do

10 They've recycled the glass bottles, ___ they?
a didn't
b haven't
c aren't

11 If I were you, I ___ the cat to the rescue centre.
a took
b take
c would take

12 Animals will die out if we ___ the environment.
a don't protect
b not protect
c didn't protect

9 Lesson 1

Vocabulary

1 Complete the dialogues with these words.

book circle dizzy magnificent passport

1 **A:** This restaurant moves round.
   B: Yes, and it makes a full _____circle_____ in four hours.

2 **A:** What's the matter with you?
   B: I feel very _____ and I want to get off this rollercoaster!

3 **A:** Let's go to the concert this Sunday.
   B: Great idea! We can _____ tickets on the Internet.

4 **A:** Welcome to Greece, sir. Could I have a look at your _____, please?
   B: Sure, here it is.

5 **A:** Look at the view!
   B: It's _____, isn't it?

2 Complete the sentences with these words.

ahead cross go right round turn

1 _____Turn_____ left at the supermarket.
2 _____ the road at the traffic lights.
3 Turn _____ at the library.
4 Go straight _____. The school is at the end of the street.
5 If you go _____ the corner, you'll see the bank on your right.
6 _____ past the park and the restaurant will be in front of you.

3 Circle the correct words.

1 Go past / ahead the traffic lights and turn right.
2 What a surprise! I didn't expect / book to see you here tonight!
3 Go round / ahead the corner and the restaurant is on your right.
4 I don't want to go on the merry-go-round because it makes me feel dizzy / magnificent.
5 Why don't we take him after / out to dinner for his birthday?
6 Go round / straight ahead and the cafe is on your left.

Grammar

4 **Complete the sentences with the correct form of** have to **and these verbs.**

book cross go not ask not do wait

1 '___Do we have to cross___ (we) the road at the traffic lights?' 'Yes, you do.'
2 We _____ tickets today if we want to fly to Seattle this Sunday.
3 We can't leave now. We _____ for Ann and Peter.
4 Sarah knew where the school was. She _____ the way.
5 I _____ my homework tonight. We've got no school tomorrow!
6 '_____ (you) to the supermarket yesterday?' 'No, I didn't need to buy anything.'

5 **Complete the sentences with** must, mustn't **or the correct form of** have to.

1 We _____must_____ leave now because Ron's waiting for us.
2 You _____ go to the bank because I went this morning.
3 You _____ drive now. The traffic light is red.
4 We don't want to miss the bus, so we _____ hurry!
5 He _____ take the metro because I can drive him to the airport.
6 You _____ go to the park, Joey! It's raining.

6 **Choose the correct answers.**

1 Do we ___ go to the travel agency today?
   a must
   ⓑ have to
   c have

2 ___ we book the tickets today? Can't we do it tomorrow?
   a Have
   b Must
   c Did

3 He ___ to turn left at Baker Street.
   a has
   b must
   c haven't

4 'Must we have our passports with us?' 'Yes, you ___.'
   a must
   b do
   c mustn't

5 You ___ go to the supermarket now. I'll do the shopping later.
   a mustn't
   b have to
   c don't have to

6 We ___ tell her about the party. It's a surprise!
   a don't have to
   b mustn't
   c must

Vocabulary

1 **The words in bold are in the wrong sentences. Write the correct words.**

1 Can I **hire** you something to drink? _____offer_____
2 This restaurant serves Japanese and **marine** food. _____
3 Did you know that Tokyo is the **tunnel** of Japan? _____
4 Water pollution can harm **international** life in the river. _____
5 I hate driving through the underground **capital** – I think it's really scary. _____
6 Let's **offer** some bikes and go cycling in the gardens. _____

2 **Complete the crossword.**

Across

4 This is a very tall building.
5 We see this in gardens and parks. It has water, but you can't swim in it!
6 This is a large open space in the centre of a city.

Down

1 This is a place where people keep their money.
2 You can buy clothes, shoes, books, toys and food in this place.
3 This is a place that you visit to see the exhibits.

3 **Complete the dialogues with these words.**

bite kite mythology pattern sightseeing

1 A: Who are Zeus and Athena?
   B: They are two of the twelve gods in Greek ____mythology____.

2 A: I could fly a _____ when I was young.
   B: Well, you can't now. Your kite has just landed in a tree!

3 A: Can we go _____ today?
   B: Sure. We can start with a visit to the Imperial Palace.

4 A: Which of these two rugs do you like?
   B: I like the colours and _____ on that one.

5 A: I'm hungry!
   B: Me too! Let's have a _____ to eat.

Grammar

4 **Complete the paragraph with** can, can't, could **or** couldn't.

Jack's really excited because he **(1)** ___can___ go on holiday with his family this year. Last year, they **(2)** _____ go anywhere because his dad had to work. Jack loves art and wants to go to New York because you **(3)** _____ visit a lot of interesting museums there, but his mum **(4)** _____ travel by plane because she's scared of flying. They will have to go somewhere by car or train. The last time they went on holiday, they went to France by train. They stayed in Paris for ten days and they **(5)** _____ see the Eiffel Tower from their hotel room. Their hotel was in the centre of the city and they **(6)** _____ walk to museums and shopping centres. They had a fantastic time, so maybe they will go back again this year.

5 **Match.**

1 You **can't** watch TV now. It's too late.
2 Of course you **can** use my laptop to check your emails.
3 **Can** I sleep over at Maria's house tonight? Please, Mum!
4 They **could** visit museums and go for long walks in the park.
5 My grandfather **could** drive a car when he was ten years old.
6 My sister is only five and she **can** read and write.

a Talking about ability in the present.
b Talking about ability in the past.
c Asking for permission.
d Giving permission.
e Not giving permission.
f Talking about possibility in the past.

6 **Answer the questions.**

1 Could you read and write when you were five years old? _____
2 Can students use their mobile phones in class? _____
3 Can children drive? _____
4 Could people send emails 200 years ago? _____
5 Could you ride a bike when you were ten months old? _____
6 Could you go to the cinema with your friends when you were nine? _____

Vocabulary

1 **Complete the sentences with these words.**

comfortable   famous   guide   right-hand   special   swimming costume

1   I shouldn't wear these shoes – they aren't ___comfortable___.
2   Don't forget your _____. We might go to the beach.
3   You'll love Toronto. It's got parks and _____ roads for cyclists.
4   We have to buy a city _____ for Paris before we leave.
5   The museum is next to the café on the _____ side of the street.
6   'What is your city _____ for?' 'Its delicious food!'

Grammar

2 **Circle the correct words.**

1   Simon should / (might) go to Egypt, but he's not sure yet.
2   You might not / shouldn't like the food in Japan.
3   She shouldn't / might not go out in the city without a guide. She'll get lost.
4   Might / Should we visit the Louvre or the Eiffel Tower first?
5   The aquarium might / should be closed on Sunday afternoons. Why don't we call and find out?
6   You should / might be careful when you walk in the city at night.
7   We shouldn't / might not go to the theatre today. We haven't decided yet.
8   Visitors might / should try Mexican food because it's delicious.

Express yourself!

3 **Complete the dialogues with these phrases.**

go past   How can I get to   How far
straight ahead   the left-hand side   turn left

Man: Excuse me. **(1)** ___How can I get to___ the bus station?

Woman: **(2)** _____ the traffic lights and turn left on Baker Street.

Woman: Do you know where the museum is?
Man: Go straight ahead and **(3)** _____ into Smithson Avenue. The museum is on **(4)** _____, after a large supermarket.

Man: **(5)** _____ is it to the park?

Woman: It's about five minutes on foot. Go **(6)** _____ on New Road. Cross the road at the traffic lights. It's on the left-hand side.

Writing

4 **Read Justin's postcard and correct any mistakes in the order of adjectives.**

Hi Chris,

How are you? I'm on holiday in a **(1) ~~Greek lovely~~** *lovely Greek* town called Galaxidi.

Galaxidi is a(n) **(2) little interesting** town by the sea with lots of things to do and see. There are **(3) clean beautiful** beaches where you can swim and there are many museums that you can visit. You can go on boat trips or you can visit Delphi with its **(4) Greek ancient amazing** temple. Delphi is only 25 kilometres from Galaxidi and you can go by bus.

Galaxidi has got **(5) beautiful stone** houses and it's ideal for those who like walking. There are some **(6) small fantastic** squares with cafés and restaurants. I had some **(7) delicious fresh** fish last night in one of the restaurants. Food here is tasty and very cheap!

You should visit Galaxidi when you come to Greece. You'll have a great time there.

See you soon!

Justin

> **Remember!**
>
> When more than one adjective comes before a noun, we put them in this order:
>
> | | |
> |---|---|
> | opinion | *brilliant* |
> | size | *huge* |
> | age | *ancient* |
> | shape | *round* |
> | colour | *orange* |
> | origin | *Greek* |
> | material | *glass* |

5 **Write a postcard to a friend describing a town. Use this plan to help you.**

Begin like this:
Hi _____ (your friend's name),

Paragraph 1
Ask your friend how he/she is. Say which town you are visiting.

Paragraph 2
Describe the town and some of the sights there.

Paragraph 3
Say what you can do/eat in the town.

Paragraph 4
Tell your friend to visit the town too.

Finish like this
See you soon!
_____ (your name)

Vocabulary

1 Complete the dialogues with these words.

artist   grow up   level   program   screen

1 **A:** How can I see this picture?

   B: Click on this button and the picture will appear on your computer _____*screen*_____.

2 **A:** What can you do with this computer _____?

   B: You can draw and colour pictures!

3 **A:** Have you thought about your future?

   B: Yes, when I _____, I want to be a computer programmer.

4 **A:** Wow! You're really good at this video game.

   B: Yes, I'm on the last _____.

5 **A:** What does your brother do?

   B: He's got a very cool job – he's a video _____.

2 Complete the crossword.

Across

3 When you do this, you make a drawing or a plan of something that you will make.

4 This is a small computer that we can carry everywhere.

5 This is on the computer monitor and it can take pictures or videos.

7 You move this with your hand to tell the computer what to do.

Down

1 This has letters, numbers and symbols on it.

2 You use this if you want to have what you see on a computer on a piece of paper.

6 This is another word for *screen*.

3 Circle the correct words.

1 Are video testers / games paid a lot of money?

2 You can't go to the third level if you don't test / complete the second level.

3 The body of the character is designed / played first.

4 They have created a new computer level / program.

5 We run a lot of tests / screens to make sure the video game is OK.

6 I prefer this screen / mouse because it moves around easily.

Grammar

4 Circle the correct words.

1 This program **is used** / used by thousands of people every day.
2 Computer games give / **are given** to teenagers so they can test them.
3 A video game isn't **played** / play like a board game.
4 Are photos take / **taken** with a web camera?
5 Computer programmers aren't **paid** / pay a lot of money.
6 Batteries **are recycled** / recycled in special recycling bins in supermarkets.
7 Are these laptops make / **made** in China?
8 **Are your friends' addresses** / Your friends' addresses are written in your diary?

5 Complete the sentences with the Present Simple Passive of the verbs in brackets.

1 Computer games _____*are tested*_____ (test) by teenagers first.
2 _____ (this program/use) to write music?
3 He _____ (know) by millions of people – he's a famous video artist.
4 These printers _____ (not make) in Japan.
5 The winners of the competition _____ (give) free tickets for the concert.
6 _____ (you/pay) for every program you design?
7 Most video games _____ (not design) for players under the age of seven.
8 J.K.Rowling's books _____ (read) by thousands of children.

6 Put the words in the correct order to make sentences.

1 invitations / the / sent / are / by email
   The invitations are sent by email.
2 computer game / by / isn't / many / played / people / this
   _____
3 characters / chosen / us / the / aren't / by
   _____
4 at / are / sold / tickets / the train station
   _____
5 ? / Bob and Jane / are / to the party / invited
   _____
6 ? / air pollution / is / caused / by / cars
   _____

Vocabulary

1 **Circle the correct words.**

1 Can I use your laptop to surf / download a video clip?
2 Did Alexander Graham Bell upload / invent the telephone?
3 Do you visit / send emails to your friend in the USA?
4 This news site is visited / surfed by thousands of people every day.
5 High-speed Internet has changed the way we communicate / receive.
6 MP3 players are a wonderful communication / invention.

2 **Write the missing letters.**

1 You do this when you are given something.   r e c e i v e
2 You use the Internet to do this with songs, video clips and films.   d _ _ _ _ _ _ _
3 You do this when you look for information on the Internet.   s _ _ _ _
4 You do this when you look at a website.   v _ _ _ _
5 You do this when you put photos on a website, so that people can see them.   u _ _ _ _ _
6 You do this when you make, design or think of a new type of thing.   i _ _ _ _ _

3 **Complete the paragraph with these words.**

| blog   communicate   design   emails   MP3 player   surf |

What do you use your computer for?

- I **(1)** _____ surf _____ the Internet when I have to do school projects.
- I write on my music **(2)** _____.
- I **(3)** _____ characters for video games.
- I receive **(4)** _____ from my friends in England.
- I download songs for my **(5)** _____.
- I **(6)** _____ with people around the world.

Could you live without your computer?

Grammar

4 Match.

1 Their new song

2 The video artist

3 These characters

4 Mobile phones

5 The testers

6 My MP3 player

a weren't told about the problem.

b was bought online.

c was recorded in a studio in New York.

d were drawn on a computer.

e were invented in the 1970s.

f was given a difficult job.

5 Complete the paragraph with the Past Simple Passive of the verbs in brackets.

Betty, La Fea or *Ugly Betty* is a famous TV programme. I download it every week and watch it on my laptop. The programme **(1)** _____ was made _____ (make) in Columbia and it **(2)** _____ (show) for the first time in 1999. Ugly Betty is not watched by people in Columbia only, however. People around the world have seen it and loved it. The character of Ugly Betty **(3)** _____ (creat) by Fernando Gaitan. Fernando wrote the story about this clever, but ugly girl who **(4)** _____ (interview) a lot of times, but couldn't get a job because her bosses didn't like the way she looked. After a lot of interviews, Betty **(5)** _____ (give) a job at a clothes company called Eco Moda. She **(6)** _____ (like) by her boss, Armando Mendoza, and got on very well with the rest of the staff. The surprising thing was that when Ugly Betty threw away her glasses and changed her hairstyle and clothes, she became a beautiful woman!

6 Complete the sentences with the Past Simple Passive of these verbs.

book   create   give   invent   not show   not take   upload

1 When _____ were _____ DVD players _____ invented _____ ?

2 That video character _____ by a team of teenagers!

3 She _____ a new laptop as a birthday present.

4 _____ the photos _____ onto your website last week?

5 All the hotel rooms _____ before the end of July last summer.

6 The TV programme _____ at the same time every week.

7 This photo _____ with a web camera.

Vocabulary

1 **Label the pictures with these words.**

car race   champion   crash   spaceship   team   wheels

1 _champion_

2 _____

3 _____

4 _____

5 _____

6 _____

Speaking

2 **Complete the table about you and your partner.**

	You	Your partner
How often do you play video games?		
What is your favourite website?		
What songs do you download?		
What video games can't you stand?		
What do you use the Internet for?		
How many computers are there in your house?		

Express yourself!

3 **Match.**

1 My favourite video game is
2 Do you prefer watching TV
3 I can't stand
4 I prefer video games
5 Who is your favourite
6 I prefer seeing films at the cinema

a to downloading them from the Internet.
b to board games.
c a car racing game called *Speed*.
d video game character?
e to surfing the Internet?
f video games!

Writing

4 Read this computer game review. Then find and correct eight spelling mistakes.

Computer games are very popular with young people. My favourite computer game is caled *Super Riders*. It is desined for everyone that likes motorcycles, even young kids! It's a simple and fan game that you can play alone or with one of your friends.

At the begining of the game, you can chouse the motorbike you want to use. Then the race starts. You use the controls to ride your motorbike. There are different races with exciting turns. Your job is to ride your motorbike as fast as you can. You have to be carefull not to hit any trees or cars. If you hit something more than three times, you loose! But you can always start a new game.

I prefer playing *Super Riders* to other computer games because it's fast and enterteining. You can play it with a friend who also likes motorbikes. You don't need to be an expert at computer games to win, so give it a try. You'll love it!

Remember!

Always read your writing and check your spelling carefully.

5 Write a review of your favourite computer game. Use this plan to help you.

Paragraph 1
Say what your favourite computer game is.

Paragraph 2
Say what happens at the beginning of the game. Say what happens after that. Say what happens at the end of the game.

Paragraph 3
Say why you prefer playing this computer game to playing other computer games.

Reading

1 Read the text about the Petronas Twin Towers.

More than nine million tourists visit Kuala Lumpur, the capital of Malaysia, every year. The Petronas Twin Towers are the symbol of Kuala Lumpur and you can see them from just about anywhere in the city. These skyscrapers are the highest twin buildings in the world.

The Towers were designed by Cesar Pelli, an Argentinean architect, and they were completed in 1998. They have got 88 floors and they are 452 metres high. There are 32,000 windows and 20 lifts in the twin buildings. There is a skybridge between the Towers on the 41st and 42nd floors. The skybridge is open to all visitors, but you must get there early if you want one of the 1,000 tickets that are given out each day.

Below the twin towers there is a shopping centre with shops that sell luxury goods, a famous concert hall for classical music, an art gallery, restaurants, cafés and a science centre. The science centre presents the history of science and technology in a fun way. It's an experience that you shouldn't miss!

2 Answer the questions.

1 What is the capital city of Malaysia?
   Kuala Lumpur

2 Who designed the Petronas Twin Towers?
   _____

3 What do you have to do if you want to go on the skybridge?
   _____

4 What can you buy at the shopping centre?
   _____

5 What can you learn about at the science centre?

Vocabulary

3 Choose the correct answers.

1 This tower moves round – it can make a full ___ in three hours!
   (a) circle
   b corner
   c square

2 You can use this computer ___ to make your own music.
   a mouse
   b monitor
   c program

3 The view from the top floor of the hotel was ___.
   a magnificent
   b dizzy
   c international

4 Go to this ___. It's got very good information for your project.
   a keyboard
   b screen
   c site

5 Welcome to Greece. Can I see your ___, please?
   a pattern
   b passport
   c e-card

6 Millions of people ___ the Internet every day.
   a surf
   b download
   c book

7 When you ___ something, you pay money so that you can use it for a short period of time.
   a hire
   b design
   c invent

8 You know a lot about technology. When you ___, you should be a programmer.
   a grow up
   b upload
   c communicate

9 The plane tickets were ___ by my dad online.
   a recorded
   b crossed
   c booked

10 Go ___ the traffic lights and turn left at the supermarket.
   a ahead
   b past
   c right

11 UNICEF is a(n) ___ organisation.
   a comfortable
   b international
   c underwater

12 I've just won. Now I can go to the next ___.
   a speed
   b level
   c tester

Grammar

4 Choose the correct answers.

1 Cindy ___ to be at the bank at 3 o'clock.
   a must
   b might
   (c) has

2 You ___ play in the fountain. It's dangerous.
   a mustn't
   b don't have to
   c couldn't

3 ___ I wear a dress to the wedding?
   a Am
   b Must
   c Have to

4 If it's a sunny day, we ___ go sightseeing.
   a might
   b have to
   c mustn't

5 'Should we leave now?' 'Yes, ___.'
   a should you
   b you shouldn't
   c you should

6 Video games ___ by a team of people.
   a designed
   b are designed
   c are designing

7 Barbara ___ sing very well when she was ten.
   a can
   b should
   c could

8 This town is visited ___ thousands of people.
   a with
   b from
   c by

9 The computer monitor ___ every morning.
   a is cleaned
   b be cleaned
   c is cleaning

10 Alexander Graham Bell ___ the laptop, did he?
   a didn't invent
   b wasn't invented
   c isn't invented

11 This documentary ___ in 2009.
   a made
   b was made
   c is made

12 Was the MP3 player ___ for John's birthday?
   a bought
   b be bought
   c was bought

Vocabulary

1 The words in bold are in the wrong sentences. Write the correct words.

1 I'll **travel** around the shopping centre for an hour and then meet you for lunch.   _____wander_____

2 What time does your **passenger** to New York leave?   _____

3 This seat isn't very **adventurous** – I think I'll sit over there.   _____

4 I don't want to **wander** by train. It's slow and tiring.   _____

5 The old lady was the only **flight** on the train from Liverpool to London.   _____

6 I don't want to go on a camel ride – I'm not a(n) **comfortable** person!   _____

2 Look at the pictures and write the missing letters.

c _h_ _e_ _c_ _k_ - _i_ _n_ d _e_ _s_ _k_

c _ _ _ _

p _ _ _ _ _ _ _ _ _

s _ _ _ b _ _ _

m _ _ _ _

m _ _ _ _ _ _ _ _

3 Complete the dialogues with these words.

> easier   more adventurous   more comfortable   more expensive   more interesting

1 **A:** Do you prefer rock climbing or swimming?

   B: I prefer rock climbing because it is _____more adventurous_____ than swimming.

2 **A:** Why did you change seats?

   B: Because this seat is _____ than that one.

3 **A:** Are you going to travel by plane or by bus?

   B: By bus. I don't want to spend a lot of money and travelling by plane is _____ than travelling by bus.

4 **A:** Is it _____ to learn to drive a car or fly a plane?

   B: Learning to drive a car! You have to train for a long time to become a pilot – it's difficult!

5 **A:** Travelling by bus is boring!

   B: You're right! I think travelling by train is _____ than travelling by bus.

Grammar

4 Choose the correct answers.

1 Martin is the ___ driver in the family.
  a good
  b better
  c best *(circled)*

2 There are ___ people on the bus today than there were yesterday.
  a more
  b many
  c most

3 My car isn't as fast ___ yours.
  a than
  b from
  c as

4 This is the ___ trip I've ever been on!
  a more exciting
  b most exciting
  c exciting

5 Metro tickets were ___ last year than they are now.
  a cheaper
  b the cheapest
  c cheap

6 Travelling by coach isn't as ___ as travelling by motorbike.
  a more tiring
  b tiring
  c most tiring

5 Circle the correct words.

1 That was the worse / worst flight of my life!
2 Walking to work is better / the best than driving.
3 What is most / the most popular means of transport in your town?
4 Bikes aren't as fast / faster as motorbikes.
5 Planes are more / most comfortable than coaches.
6 These are the cheaper / cheapest tickets we could find on the Internet.

6 Complete the sentences with the correct comparative or superlative form and the adjectives in brackets.

1 Is travelling by plane ___*safer than*___ travelling by train? (safe)
2 The weather today isn't as ___ it was yesterday. (bad)
3 This is ___ film I've ever seen. (frightening)
4 Is this ___ printer in the shop? (cheap)
5 Visiting a museum is ___ going to a shopping centre. (interesting)
6 Is that ___ seat on the train? (comfortable)

Vocabulary

1 Write the missing letters.

1 This is when you have enough money to pay for something.   a _f_ _f_ _o_ _r_ _d_

2 This is a long seat for two or more people.   b _ _ _ _ _

3 Horses pulled this and it carried passengers.   c _ _ _ _ _

4 This is a trip – usually a long one.   j _ _ _ _ _ _ _

5 This is how most people feel when they are on a plane
   for many hours.   u _ _ _ _ _ _ _ _ _ _ _ _

6 This is someone who steals things.   t _ _ _ _ _

2 Complete the crossword.

Across

1 This is a set of moving stairs.

5 This is where you can buy your ticket at a station.

7 This person checks tickets on a bus or train.

Down

2 This is something you see in the street that gives you information.

3 These are suitcases and bags that you carry when you travel.

4 This has a list of the times at which buses, trains, planes, etc arrive and leave.

6 This is one of the parts of the train where passengers sit.

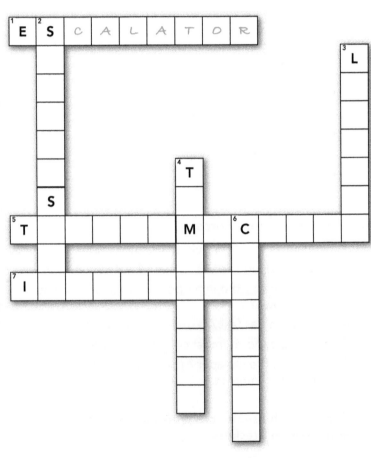

3 Write M (means of transport) or T (things related to means of transport).

1 ticket machine	T	6 metro	☐
2 tram	☐	7 train	☐
3 coach	☐	8 seat	☐
4 bench	☐	9 bus	☐
5 dining car	☐	10 timetable	☐

Grammar

4 Look at the train timetable and write T (true) or F (false).

From	To	Leaves at	Arrives at	Length of journey	Comments
Madrid (Atocha Station)	Seville (Santa Justa Station)	7:00	9:30	2 hours and 30 minutes	runs Monday – Friday
Madrid (Atocha Station)	Barcelona (Sants Station)	7:30	10:50	3 hours and 20 minutes	runs every day
Madrid (Atocha Station)	Cordoba (Central)	6:30	8:20	1 hour and 50 minutes	runs Monday – Friday
Madrid (Chamartin Station)	Barcelona (Sants Station)	22:20	7:20	9 hours	runs every day

1 You can get a train to Barcelona from both Atocha Station and Chamartin Station. **T**
2 Neither of the trains to Barcelona runs on a Sunday. ☐
3 You can travel to either Cordoba or Barcelona from Chamartin. ☐
4 Both trains to Barcelona leave in the morning. ☐
5 You can't arrive in either Seville or Cordoba before 8 o'clock. ☐
6 Neither the journey to Seville nor the journey to Cordoba takes more than two and a half hours. ☐

5 Choose the correct answers.

1 ___ the ticket machines nor the escalators work.
  a Neither
  b Either
  c Both

2 We can travel either by tram ___ by bus into town.
  a nor
  b and
  c or

3 You can book tickets for ___ trains and planes online.
  a neither
  b both
  c either

4 You can take the metro to ___ Bond Street or Liverpool Street from here.
  a neither
  b both
  c either

5 ___ the number 64 bus and the number 19 bus go past the museum.
  a Neither
  b Both
  c Either

6 The city has got neither trains ___ trams.
  a nor
  b and
  c or

6 Complete the paragraph with both, either or neither. Sometimes more than one answer is possible.

The Museum of Transport is very popular **(1)** ___both___ with the people from the town and tourists. There are two big exhibitions at the museum – one about passenger trains and one about the history of air travel. You can visit **(2)** _____ of them from 9 am to 5 pm from Monday to Friday. You can **(3)** _____ go on a tour with a guide or look at the different means of transport on your own. Sadly, **(4)** _____ exhibition is open at the weekends, but you can visit the museum on Saturday mornings and listen to an interesting talk about **(5)** _____ the history of train travel or solar cars of the future. Don't miss **(6)** _____ of these talks. They're fantastic!

Vocabulary

1 **Match.**

1 How much is a return
2 Where can I get a water
3 How much is a travel
4 Where is the nearest bus
5 How often does the metro

a run at weekends?
b station?
c ticket to Oxford?
d bus to Saint Marc's Square?
e pass for one day?

Grammar

2 **Circle the correct words.**

1 There aren't too many / **enough** tickets for everyone. We need two more.
2 This tram is going **enough** / too fast!
3 The bus is crowded – there are **too many** / enough people on it.
4 She was **too** / enough tired to go sightseeing.
5 The bus crashed because the driver wasn't careful too / **enough**.
6 We can't get the tram now. It's **too late** / late enough.

Express yourself!

3 **Complete the dialogues with these questions.**

Can I buy a single ticket to Duke Street, please?   Can I buy a travel pass, please?
Can I travel to the island by boat?   Excuse me, how can I get to Hope Street?
Where do I get off for the Transport Museum?

1 **Man:** _Excuse me, how can I get to Hope Street?_
Woman: You can take the bus from the stop in Wellington Street.

2 **Boy:** _____
Man: Yes. A single ticket costs £1.40.

3 **Woman:** _____
Man: Yes. A travel pass costs £55 for one month.

4 **Girl:** _____
Man: You get off at the next stop.

5 **Man:** _____
Woman: Yes. You can take the ferry from the port at one o'clock.

Writing

4 **The headings in the report below are in the wrong places.**
Read the report and put the headings in the correct place.

(1) Timetable _Tourists in the summer_

At the moment, not many ferries come to our island. For this reason, most tourists prefer visiting other islands where they can go by ferry or water taxi. Our island has fewer tourists in the summer than other islands.

(2) Cost _____

You can only get to our island by ferry either very early in the morning or late at night, and this isn't easy for passengers. There are no ferries to our island at the weekend.

(3) What can we do? _____

Another problem with travelling by ferry is the price of tickets. The cost of return tickets is too high. For some journeys, the cost of return ferry tickets is the same as the cost of plane tickets!

(4) Tourists in the summer _____

Travelling by ferry can become more popular if we change some things. Firstly, we can change the times of ferries and make sure some leave during the day. We can also have special prices for groups of people and make return tickets cheaper. I think these changes will make travelling by ferry more popular.

Remember!

When you write a report, put a heading above each part. The heading should tell the reader what each part is about.

5 **Write a report about the problems with a means of transport in your city. Use this plan to help you.**

Paragraph 1
Say what means of transport you are going to talk about and say that it could be better.

Paragraph 2
Say what one of the problems is and talk about why this is a problem.

Paragraph 3
Say what another problem is and talk about why this is a problem.

Paragraph 4
Suggest ways to deal with the problems.

Vocabulary

1 **Complete the sentences with these words.**

admire   follow   grab   panic   rescue   slip

1 Be careful! You might _____slip_____ on the wet floor!
2 This programme is about a group of people who _____ people in danger.
3 Don't _____! I'll go and get some help!
4 Here! _____ my hand and I'll pull you up.
5 I _____ people who think about other people first, don't you?
6 You can connect the printer to the computer if you _____ these instructions carefully.

2 **Complete the crossword.**

Across

4 This person works on your car or motorbike when it has a problem.
6 This person takes pictures and works for a magazine or newspaper.

Down

1 This person finds information and then catches thieves.
2 This person works on a ship.
3 This person draws or paints pictures.
5 This person is the main cook in a restaurant.
7 This person saves people's lives.

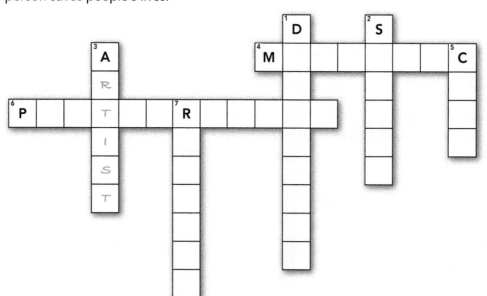

3 **Match.**

1 Thank you! You saved   a the cliff!
2 We are rescuers. We work   b our instructions.
3 Oh no! That climber is going to fall down   c my life!
4 If you want us to help you, you must follow   d as a team.
5 I'd love to see the rescuers   e panic.
6 Stay calm. You mustn't   f in action.

Grammar

4 **Circle the correct words.**

1 How quick / **quickly** can you finish this?
2 I didn't sleep good / well last night.
3 That's a beautiful / beautifully painting.
4 The children ate the sandwiches hungry / hungrily.
5 The detective found the thief easy / easily.
6 The angry / angrily taxi driver got out of his car and started shouting.
7 That cliff looks dangerous / dangerously.

5 **Complete the job advert with adverbs made from the adjectives in brackets.**

Chef wanted for yacht

Do you love travelling, but can't afford a holiday this year? Can you cook
(1) _____well_____ (good) even for the most difficult people? Can you cook for
people who eat **(2)** _____ (healthy) but like exotic food? Can you learn
(3) _____ (quick)? Then you can be one of the chefs on *Ocean Dream*.
Our chefs work **(4)** _____ (hard) every day. They make food
(5) _____ (fast) but **(6)** _____ (careful). Our chefs work
(7) _____ (happy) together as a team. If you enjoy cooking and
travelling on a boat, you'll love this job.

Give us a call now!

6 **Answer the questions.**

1 What do you always do wrong?   _____
2 What do you always do right?   _____
3 Who works hard in your family?   _____
4 Who drives badly in your family?   _____
5 What food do you eat hungrily?   _____
6 What do you and your friends do lazily? _____

Vocabulary

1 Choose the correct answers.

1 conservationist
   (a) someone who works to protect plants and animals
   b someone who travels in tropical countries

2 involve
   a be an important part of something
   b be exciting

3 endangered species
   a animals that live in the jungle
   b animals that will probably die out

4 incredible
   a extremely good, large or great
   b bad and unpleasant

5 look for signs
   a make plans
   b find events or facts that give information

2 Circle the correct words.

1 Rwanda is a fantastic country to explore / involve.
2 Mr Jones is the manager / employee and has a staff of twenty people.
3 He has a lot of career / experience – he has worked in restaurants in Paris and New York.
4 A conservationist / biologist works to protect animals and plants.
5 What can we do to prevent / protect air pollution?

3 Complete the dialogues with these words.

   dead   full-time   member   part-time   population   qualifications

1 **A:** Are you looking for a ____full-time____ job?
   B: Yes, I am. I have no problem working eight hours every day.

2 **A:** Is that little bird _____?
   B: No, it isn't. It's moving its wings.

3 **A:** Do you think he will get the job?
   B: I don't think so. He didn't go to college and hasn't got any _____.

4 **A:** Tell me about your new job, Steve.
   B: Well, it's a _____ job – I work on Friday evenings and Saturday mornings.

5 **A:** Is he a _____ of the school staff?
   B: Yes, he teaches science.

6 **A:** Is it true that the _____ of big cats is getting smaller?
   B: Yes, conservationists believe that there will be no big cats in 10 to 15 years.

Grammar

4 Match.

1 This is the man
2 I worked in a travel agent's
3 We had dinner in a restaurant
4 Bristol is the city
5 That's the artist
6 I've bought a mobile phone

a which can send and receive emails.
b where people came to buy plane tickets.
c whose paintings you can see at the exhibition.
d which was by the sea.
e who manages the hotel.
f where I grew up.

5 Complete the sentences with who, which **or** where **and these words and phrases.**

~~are~~ has live they spent we found works

1 I don't like people _____ who are _____ rude.
2 Big cats are animals _____ in the wild.
3 This is the beach _____ the coins under the sand.
4 Heather is a hairdresser _____ for eight hours every day.
5 This is the island _____ their summer holiday last year.
6 They live in a house _____ a pool and a big garden.

6 Put the words in the correct order to make sentences.

1 teachers / schools / people / in / who / work / are
___Teachers are people who work in schools.___

2 restaurant / John / where / that's / works / the
_____

3 Sheila / which / job / she / a / really / has / enjoys / got
_____

4 eight / creatures / legs / which / are / spiders / have
_____

5 chefs / are / where / restaurants / places / work
_____

6 which / take / school / rucksack / the / I / to / is / this
_____

Vocabulary

1 Circle the correct words.

1 You have to go to university / a rescue centre to become a vet.

2 Pilots must have a lot of career / skills.

3 I am very interested in / at computer programming.

4 He wants to be a farmer because he likes working outdoors / indoors.

5 You're good at selling / fixing things – you should be a mechanic.

6 She wants to study / apply for the job of hotel manager.

Express yourself!

2 Complete the dialogue with these words.

explaining fixing helping qualifications skills working

Brian: Greg, have you thought about your future? Do you know what you want to be when you grow up?

Greg: I want to be a teacher because I'm very good at (1) _explaining_ things. I also enjoy (2) _____ people understand new ideas.

Brian: You will have to go to university first because teachers must have (3) _____.

Greg: Yes, I know. You have to study for four years to become a teacher.

Brian: Do you get on with children?

Greg: I love (4) _____ with children. I've also got very good computer (5) _____ which are helpful for teachers. I think I'll be a good teacher. Have you got any idea what you want to do? What are you good at?

Brian: Well, I'm very good at (6) _____ machines, so I might become a mechanic.

Greg: Yes, that's a good idea.

Speaking

3 Talk to your partner about the job you want to do. Explain what qualifications and skills you need for this job and what is good and bad about it.

Writing

4 Read the article below and complete the notes with the main ideas from the article.

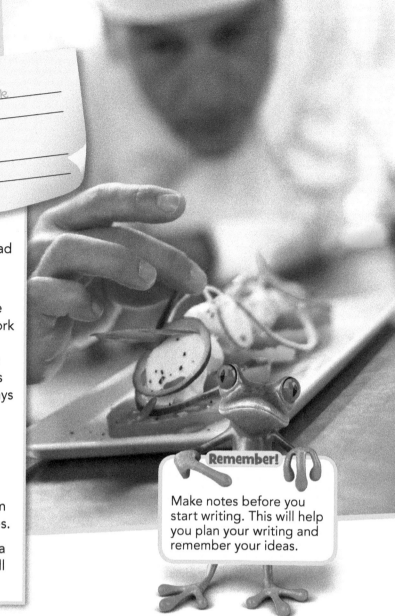

Worst part:
tiring work

_____

Best part:

_____

_____

My Ideal Job

I've always wanted to be a chef, so I got a part-time job in an Italian restaurant. I now know that there are some good things and some bad things about being a chef.

First of all, I didn't know that working in the kitchen of a restaurant was so tiring. You have to work really fast but very carefully. Chefs work long hours in a place which is very hot. You have to stand up for hours and that gives you sore feet and a sore back. Another problem is that chefs often work at weekends and holidays too.

However, not everything was bad. I really enjoyed working with the people in the restaurant and I spoke to different kinds of people. Another good thing about it was the experience. I learned a lot about cooking from other chefs and I even created my own recipes.

I got some good experience from working in a restaurant and I know that I can do the job. All I need now are the qualifications!

Remember!

Make notes before you start writing. This will help you plan your writing and remember your ideas.

5 Write an article which talks about the good and bad parts of a job. Use this plan to help you.

Paragraph 1
Introduction: Say what job you are going to write about and that there are good and bad things about it.

Paragraph 2
Write about the bad things and explain why they are bad.

Paragraph 3
Write about the good things and explain why they are good.

Paragraph 4
Conclusion: End your article.

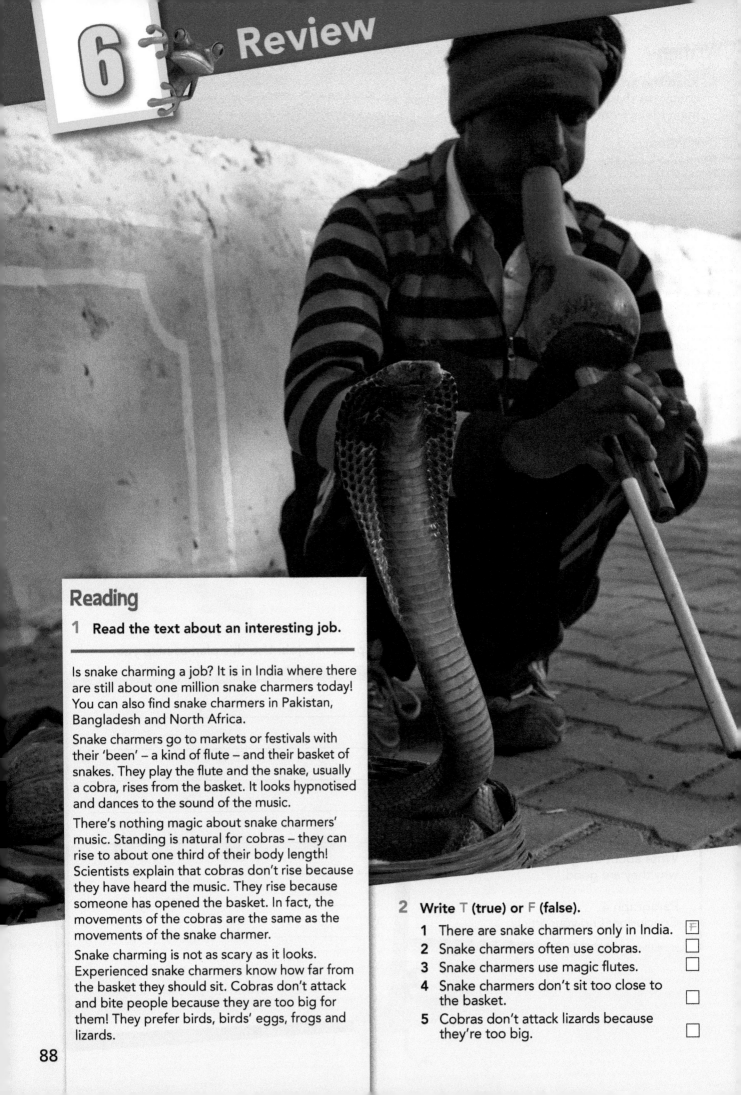

Reading

1 Read the text about an interesting job.

Is snake charming a job? It is in India where there are still about one million snake charmers today! You can also find snake charmers in Pakistan, Bangladesh and North Africa.

Snake charmers go to markets or festivals with their 'been' – a kind of flute – and their basket of snakes. They play the flute and the snake, usually a cobra, rises from the basket. It looks hypnotised and dances to the sound of the music.

There's nothing magic about snake charmers' music. Standing is natural for cobras – they can rise to about one third of their body length! Scientists explain that cobras don't rise because they have heard the music. They rise because someone has opened the basket. In fact, the movements of the cobras are the same as the movements of the snake charmer.

Snake charming is not as scary as it looks. Experienced snake charmers know how far from the basket they should sit. Cobras don't attack and bite people because they are too big for them! They prefer birds, birds' eggs, frogs and lizards.

2 Write T (true) or F (false).

1 There are snake charmers only in India. [F]
2 Snake charmers often use cobras. ☐
3 Snake charmers use magic flutes. ☐
4 Snake charmers don't sit too close to the basket. ☐
5 Cobras don't attack lizards because they're too big. ☐

Vocabulary

3 **Choose the correct answers.**

1 If you're hungry, we can go to the ___ and have lunch.
   (a) dining car
   b ticket machine
   c seat belt

2 Both of my parents are ___ at a French restaurant in the city.
   a mechanics
   b sailors
   c chefs

3 My ___ is faster than yours, but yours is newer.
   a tram
   b metro
   c motorbike

4 These are the ___ which you need to get the job.
   a members
   b qualifications
   c means

5 We had a lot of ___ because we were going to be away for a month.
   a transport
   b luggage
   c timetables

6 I have a ___ job. I only work on Mondays and Wednesdays.
   a crowded
   b full-time
   c part-time

7 That's my ___ brother who loves surfing and snorkelling!
   a adventurous
   b comfortable
   c uncomfortable

8 That's the ___ who will look at our bus tickets.
   a escalator
   b inspector
   c thief

9 Here! ___ my hand or you will fall off the tram!
   a Grab
   b Slip
   c Prevent

10 Don't ___! I'll find someone to help us.
   a admire
   b panic
   c rescue

11 That's the ___ where we have to show our passports.
   a ticket machine
   b street sign
   c check-in desk

12 You have neither the skills nor the ___ to become the manager.
   a staff
   b career
   c experience

Grammar

4 **Choose the correct answers.**

1 Craig is the ___ mechanic in this town!
   a bad
   (b) worst
   c worse

2 Taking the bus is ___ than taking a taxi.
   a too cheap
   b cheapest
   c cheaper

3 They're going on a journey ___ starts in two weeks.
   a which
   b who
   c where

4 This is one of the artist's ___ paintings.
   a nicest
   b most nice
   c nicer than

5 My job isn't as interesting ___ yours.
   a than
   b as
   c then

6 Is this the drawer ___ you put the plane tickets?
   a who
   b which
   c where

7 I can't afford first class tickets. They're ___.
   a too expensive
   b expensive enough
   c as expensive

8 We can travel ___ by bus or by plane.
   a neither
   b either
   c nor

9 I can't travel to Japan. I've got neither the money ___ the time.
   a and
   b or
   c nor

10 This carriage isn't ___ for all these people.
   a bigger
   b big enough
   c too big

11 The coach shouted ___ at the players.
   a angry
   b angriest
   c angrily

12 That's the car ___ hit me.
   a who
   b where
   c which

Crossword puzzles

Units 1–2

Across

1 Tom and his _____, Alice, are Peter's parents.
4 You can put all your clothes in a _____.
6 What's the _____ from your house to the park?
8 William Shakespeare lived in the 16th _____.
9 Mum is away and I really _____ her!

Down

2 I need a new bed and other _____ for my bedroom.
3 It isn't _____ to ride a motorbike without a helmet!
5 She used a _____ cleaner to clean the rug.
7 'My _____, David, is my uncle's son.'

Units 3 – 4

Across

1 I need some water. I'm so _____.

4 A _____ tells you how to cook something.

5 Everyone wants to be in his films. He's a _____ director.

8 I'm not very good at dancing. I need to _____ more.

9 A _____ is a small mountain.

Down

2 I haven't had anything to eat since yesterday, so I'm _____!

3 She's great at ice-skating – she won the ice-skating _____.

5 Can I have some sugar in my coffee, please? I don't like it _____.

6 The Chinese _____ lived in a palace.

7 Don't feel bad. It was not your _____.

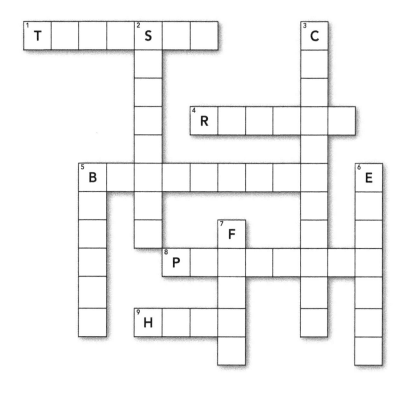

Crossword puzzles

Units 5 – 6

Across

1 He had a good _____. He went to an excellent university.
4 The people of this _____ live in the Amazon.
5 I feel ill. I've got a _____ throat.
6 This spider is the largest I've ever seen. It's really _____!
8 People shouldn't go to _____; they should live in peace.
9 The school _____ has more than 2,000 books you can read.

Down

2 You feel hot. You must have a _____.
3 I hit my _____ on the table and now I can't walk!
5 Don't go too close to the bird, you will _____ it away.
7 She's not here these days, she's travelling _____.

Units 7 – 8

Across

2 It is better to wash this red shirt _____.

4 A strong wind blew and all the _____ from the trees fell on the ground.

5 Turn off the tap when you _____ your teeth to save water.

6 She took her old cans and bottles for _____.

7 They cut a large _____ off the tree.

8 Please throw this in the _____ bin.

9 I'll be with you in just a _____.

Down

1 Energy from the sun is called _____ energy.

3 Pollution of the _____ is a serious problem for everyone on our planet.

5 There was a _____ star shining in the night sky.

93

Crossword puzzles

Units 9 – 10

Across

2 Thousands of visitors go to the top of the mountain to see the _____ view.

4 They didn't bring their own car, so they _____ a car for a few days.

7 The last two _____ of this video game are very hard.

8 I don't buy CDs any longer, I _____ all my music from the Internet.

10 Don't turn left or right, just walk _____ ahead.

Down

1 We saw all kinds of _____ life at the Sea Park.

3 Millions of people use text messages to _____ with each other.

5 Rome is the _____ of Italy.

6 Don't forget to take your _____ with you to the airport – you can't fly without it.

9 I don't want to go on the rollercoaster! It makes me feel _____.

Units 11 – 12

Across

3 They managed to _____ the man from the burning building and save his life.

4 A moving staircase that you often find in shopping centres or airports is called an _____ .

7 The airplane is the fastest _____ of transport.

9 He couldn't _____ to buy a new car, so he bought a second-hand one.

10 The _____ of wild tigers has got much smaller in the last 20 years.

Down

1 People love and _____ him for his work as an explorer.

2 They asked people not to drive in the snow to _____ accidents from happening.

5 She was going away for a whole year, so she had a lot of _____ to check in.

6 She likes to _____ around the mall without buying anything.

8 Passengers must wear their _____ during take-off and landing.